A CONTEMPORARY MYSTICISM

VIS

If invisible,

I could serve as window

to the other side.

With nonbeing,

a door.

Michael Resman

A CONTEMPORARY MYSTICISM

Support on the Spiritual Path

MICHAEL RESMAN

ISBN 978-0692370148

Published by
Zumbro River Press LLC
Rochester, Minnesota

On the cover – Photograph taken by the author
while on a prayer walk in Oxbow Park, along the
banks of the Zumbro River

I am not a saint, but I know of no more worthy goal.

(unknown)

CONTENTS

INTRODUCTION TO THE INTRODUCTION

This book is quite informal, even chatty. Some might think that's inappropriate for a sacred subject. But what else could it be? Spiritual journeys can only be shared as stories, told by one traveler to another.

This conversation is necessarily one sided, but perhaps someday we will meet face to face. Then, after we've taken the measure of each other and develop some trust and recognition, I can hear your stories of life on the other side.

For these come from a tender place. They are, after all, love stories. Tales of a weak, limited person who fell completely in love with God. When the veil is pulled aside, no matter how briefly, and we behold that great Love, how else could we respond?

And like all love stories, they are filled with ecstasy, growth, loss, confusion and failures. Messy, individual and entirely personal, these experiences come to form the core of life.

1

You'd think that being able to hang out with God would be enough – in fact more than anyone could ever expect in this earthly life. But no, being human we long to share with others.

Many people are touched by God. Few westerners know someone they can talk with when it happens. Even with God as a companion, we feel isolated from other people. If only there were someone who could guide, console, support or celebrate what we're experiencing.

That's what this book is for. These stories are crumbs, dropped here and there on the path. I hope they provide reassurance that others have been where you're going and some hints of what you could look for as you continue on.

So, imagine we're sitting around a fire somewhere in the wilderness. Faces intermittently illuminated by flames, we watch random sparks lift to a black, silent sky. Stories are exchanged of steep climbs and treacherous slopes; getting lost and being found. Boundless joy and agony; seeing all and nothing; soaring through the universe and falling flat on our face.

Between brushing off mosquitoes and waving the smoke away we listen, open our hearts, and if we're lucky, touch each other's soul.

INTRODUCTION

Almost twenty years ago, I had an epiphany experience. During a time of emotional crises, I was lifted to heaven and was fully in the presence of God. That brief experience placed me on a spiritual path that continues to this day.

While it has been wonderfully enriching and transforming, I have also had to struggle to understand what was happening, and have been haunted by doubts about whether I was proceeding as I should. At times, I was afraid that I was going crazy and was wracked by an awareness of what a deeply flawed and unworthy creature I am. I have also known boundless peace, wrapped in the arms of the One.

Throughout it all, I have had to keep my own counsel. There was simply no one near who could understand what I was going through. I found little to read that was helpful, and for months didn't even have a term for what had happened. During prayer walks in state parks I wandered alone, calling out to God for guidance. While I was sometimes comforted, I was also brought to the brink of despair.

All these years, I longed for a companion. Someone who had spent more time on the spiritual path, who could teach me, provide a context or warnings, and keep me from falling. For that was my greatest fear, that I would mess up so thoroughly that God would give up on me.

This book is intended to speak to that need in others. There is not a shred of "fact" here, merely stories of triumph and tribulation, hope and fear, ecstasy and agony. The title speaks to its limitation. This is only "A" contemporary mysticism – one person's journey. Whether it has any relevance for your life is up to you to decide.

As a Quaker, it is my sincere desire that you don't believe a word I say. Instead, I hope you take bits and pieces presented here into your mind, heart and soul to discover your own truth. That to me is the essence of Quaker spirituality.

While I am thus able to stay true to my own religious tradition, it's my assumption that you will stay true to yours. Quakers rarely proselytize, in fact we do a pretty good job of hiding ourselves. We may be out there promoting social justice causes, but quietly gather on Sunday morning doing who else knows what.

Rest assured, this book is not an effort to convince you that your religious background is wrong. My intent is to support your spiritual – interior – life. Once you're "plugged in", I'm certain you will see, as others have throughout the ages, that the outward trappings of religions are just that – trappings. Your soul and mine are connected to each other and all others. Differences of language, culture, economics and personal histories exist between us. Nonetheless, when we look at each other with our spiritual eyes, it is clear we are all one.

These stories come from my own experience. I am almost entirely ignorant of the Bible, philosophy or theology. In addition to what I experienced, I've included conclusions I've reached. I needed to process what was going on, in order to put things in a bigger perspective. Doing that allowed my thinking self to catch up with what my soul experienced and allowed me to move ahead into further strange and paradoxical waters. I've included those thoughts for you.

The image comes to mind that I am like a frog, leaping from one lily pad to the next. Unaware of what goes on below me, unable to see very far ahead and always having to work to maintain my balance. Sometimes missing or falling off, and having to climb back up. I hope my conclusions provide some places for you to land, and support you as you move on.

I've also included poems, sprinkled about the text where they seemed relevant, and at the end. They are reports of visions and understandings that have come to me. There are many human experiences that can't really be put into words – the color red, or the love of a mother for a child. Still less can we express the reality of an encounter with God. Poetry for me creates some space between the words where perhaps some tiny bits of truth can leak out.

My initial epiphany experience was intense, and I was yanked onto the spiritual path. I have talked with many people who are climbing the hill more slowly. I can share what I've learned from that more gradual process, but this book is necessarily colored by what happened to me. Please use it as a travel guide.

I often reflect on the line in the Declaration of Independence about having the right to the "pursuit of happiness". We may have the right, but it is a fruitless quest. Happiness, whether based on success, wealth or relationships is not only finite but fragile. It must come to an end. If nothing else destroys our happiness, death puts an end to all earthly pursuits.

Instead of happiness we'll share here about joy, a joy so deep that it transcends life's trials; so strengthening that it enables one to embrace suffering. The spiritual gifts that flow from living a renunciate life will be discussed, including serenity – rarely talked about but wonderfully comforting.

Through the trials and failures on the spiritual path and the aching bone deep pain of one's unworthiness comes companionship. I've come to love solitude, for I can never be alone. What a marvelous antidote to the isolation and loneliness so many feel in our modern society – the presence of God.

Just the same, I offer no false promises. Great evil has been done by those who promised that they could bring others to God. We'll discuss the issue in more depth, but what happened to me was God's will, not my doing. What happens to you will be the same.

There are no guarantees in a spiritual life, except: God loves you. God is always present and will never move away from you.

Your task is to pay attention. Just that. Give God your attention. How simple; and impossible.

DEFINITIONS

A dictionary definition of mysticism includes the phrase "…a direct intimate union of the soul with God". [1] It's that simple. And wonderful. Despite this simplicity, misperceptions abound. They include:

It could only happen to a Saint.

If it ever happened, it doesn't anymore.

It's impossible because God is unknowable.

God wouldn't connect so thoroughly to an individual.

If it did happen to someone they would go mad, (or they would become perfect).

No one would believe it had happened.

The things such a person would say are nonsense.

The things such a person would say are vitally important.

I don't believe any of those things. I claim to have seen heaven, and to have been briefly in the

---

[1] Webster's New Universal Unabridged Dictionary

presence of God. I have heard the voice of God on several occasions, and continue to have visions while in prayer, when it suits God's purpose.

It happened to me, an ordinary – and as you'll see a flawed - person.

The totality of God is unknowable. However, God appears in a way most useful to us. These small, limited manifestations are knowable. After all, if we had no understanding of what had happened to us, what would be the point?

I didn't go mad, but I was confused and wondered whether I had. My experience was transforming and enabled me to become more loving and spiritual. God chose to come to a very limited person, so while I was "better", the idea of my being perfect is laughable.

I've been very careful who I told. For the first six months, I told no one. Now, I rarely need to. Other spiritual people quickly recognize a fellow traveler without having to exchange spiritual autobiographies. I stay in the "spiritual closet" around those who aren't open.

I surely was inarticulate for years after my initial experience. I am perfectly capable of saying silly, dumb things.

The relevance of a mystic's experience in the lives of others varies. A mystic's comment could pierce one listener, while boring the person sitting next to them. It all depends.

Now, how are you supposed to react when you hear someone say things like this? I can't remember how many religious leaders I've heard stating that, "We can't know what heaven is like." But here I am, saying, "I know. I've been there. Let me tell you what I discovered."

An almost universal reaction to my statement would be, "Whoa, wait a minute. I'm not ready to believe that." Particularly if you can't look into my eyes and judge the tone of my voice, skepticism is only natural.

I'd like to offer the following metaphor to use in examining the concept of mysticism. It deliberately excludes any notion of religion or spirituality, so we can examine interpersonal aspects of the experience.

Imagine a lecture hall. The students have entered from the back door. The lecturer asks for a volunteer, and a girl sitting to the side raises her hand. She is given the following instructions. "Please go out the side door and turn to your left. You will see a blue note card taped to the wall. Read what is written on it. Return to your seat without letting us know what was written on the card, or even whether there was a card." The student – let's call her Sally – does so.

Once she's performed the task and returned to her seat, Sally is different from the rest of the students. She has had an experience and has information that the other students haven't.

If the students were polled about whether they thought there was a card, and if so what it said, they would be operating on the basis of belief. Sally on the other hand would not believe whether there was a card, she would know. Her knowledge would have come to her through her brain's interpretation of a sensory experience. We thus see a clear distinction between believing and knowing.

When Sally reports her findings, the other students will judge her statement based on several factors.

Was Sally able to accurately understand her experience? What if she was color blind and mistook a yellow card for a blue one? What if she was visually impaired, and had difficulty making out the writing on the card? Perhaps the card was written in a language she didn't fully understand.

Is Sally telling the truth? For reasons such as power or influence, has she distorted what she experienced? Is she holding information back?

How important is her information for other students? Should they remember what she says? Check it out for themselves or simply ignore it?

After Sally gives her report, what has changed? Until other students have an opportunity to get up and check the hallway, Sally remains the only one with direct information. The others can believe or not believe her based on their evaluation of her competence and accuracy.

The contents of her report and student's judgment of her veracity will determine what importance they place on what she said. If she reports for example that the answers for next weeks' test are posted, her information will assume significant importance. If she reports that the card not only gave the test answers, but that it told her to tear the card up and keep the information to herself, she gains status. If she wishes to use her knowledge, offering it for sale, she has gained advantage and power as well.

If all that was written on the card were instructions to turn off the lights at the end of the lecture, Sally's experience is of little value – or importance - to the others. If the card proclaims that Sally is the long lost daughter of the last Czar, her report will be widely rejected as nonsense.

Thus it is with reports of mystical experiences. The individual can offer no proof but claims a direct knowledge. Those hearing it must evaluate the speaker's competence, motives and veracity. Chances are, each recipient of the story will come to a conclusion that is highly individual. Story telling is after all a complex interplay between speaking and hearing. Each member of the audience will bring their particular history, understandings, openness and needs to bear, filtering and interpreting what they hear.

But what if Sally went out the door and read the card, turned to go back inside, and God was standing there. In some manner she could readily discern, it was unquestionably God. Surely, an encounter with such an extraordinary presence would transform Sally and become the central event of her life.

Odds are, the other people in the lecture hall would notice a difference in Sally when she returned. She would probably appear dazed, confused and radiant. If asked what she'd seen, if she chose to speak, her explanation would probably seem simplistic and inarticulate. These are the hallmarks I expect in someone who was recently been touched by God – mundane images that are transformative and overwhelming, and an inability to clearly articulate what happened. It took me over a decade before I could express what happened with any coherence.

Non-mystics may expect images of God that are dramatic – a burning bush, or bright light and booming voice. Maybe a holographic kind of three dimensional Jesus who looks like the paintings. Instead, they hear about a drop of water or a falling leaf. We also expect competent witnesses to tell an adequate story – linking events we can comprehend in a linear fashion. Not stumbling phrases that seem to have little connection.

But Sally's life has been turned upside down. Much of what she was certain was true about herself as well as the physical and spiritual world will have to be relearned. Emotionally, she has a new center that has altered and displaced all her relationships with family, friends and all the people of the world. The very meaning of life and death have been transformed.

More importantly, she is overwhelmed with love. Her soul, of which she was barely aware, is now brimming over with peace, love, joy, ecstasy – Grace. It's a marvel that so much of God's love can fit inside her.

While she may wonder at first if this is real and if she has gone crazy, every particle of her confirms that it's true. It happened. It was God. This new knowing supplants the old. As certain as she can feel the ground beneath her feet and the breeze on her cheek, she met God. And everything is gloriously different.

All this in the space of a few minutes. No wonder Sally is dazed.

On those few occasions when I have talked with a friend or relative who is not spiritually oriented, my comments have been met with puzzlement. Mysticism simply doesn't fit within a typical religious context.

You mean they were born again? Is that what a mystic is talking about? My understanding is that a born again experience is intensely emotional, involving an act of will and faith. Those who are born again dedicate themselves to God, and live according to their beliefs.

Faith is the foundation of religion. An understanding of God is provided through reading and the teachings of religious leaders. Belief grows that there is a God, heaven, hell and in the right actions to live and worship. Adherents fervently believe and live their lives accordingly. This is hard work - making sacrifices, working hard because you think you should.

Mystics have it much easier. They <u>know</u>. God is as real as the wind or sunlight. I can no more deny God's existence then my own. I go through life comforted, companioned, guided in ways that I can see. I have to work very hard sometimes to understand, and often struggle to carry out what I'm to do, but put no effort into believing.

People who are only religious have great difficulty comprehending the difference. They may sing the words from the hymn In the Garden[2], "And he walks with me, and he talks with me, And he tells me I am his own; And the joy we share as we tarry there, None other has ever known." When I say that this is my favorite hymn, because God <u>does</u> walk with me and talk with me, it doesn't compute. The hymn for them is a metaphor. It isn't supposed to be real, can't be.

They are already doing what they understand is the best way to honor and follow God. Since what I'm talking about is outside of what anyone within their religion speaks about, it can't be right.

But it is real for me. I haven't found a way to bridge that gap in understanding.

---

[2] In the Garden, C. Austin Miles

BACKGROUND

Human history is full of reports of direct connections between people and the Divine. In the West, the Old Testament records numerous examples on God speaking to someone and intervening directly in lives. The story of Saul and Pentecost are examples in the New Testament.

As Christianity developed, mysticism became an accepted part of some branches. Monks and nuns, saints and hermits were often thought to be divinely connected. Religions developed that incorporated mysticism. Shakers, at least for a time, accepted direct revelation as an accepted path to truth. Mormonism was founded from heavenly visions. Quakers continue to expect that God will speak to them directly, personally.

So what happened? You could go from one mainstream Christian church to another, and it would be clear that instances of God "walking the earth" are history. Relegated perhaps to rare instances like Mother Theresa. Interesting to read about, but not happening now.

There is a difference between religion and spirituality. There need not be any conflict or tension between them, but the difference should be understood. Spirituality is the relationship of one soul with the Divine. It is internal, personal, idiosyncratic. Just as the relationship between any two people is unique, so are the relationships each person develops with God. There will be many similarities between what people report, but differences as well. These are two individuals in love.

Religion is the external, visible practice of worship by more than one person. Imagine that two people meet and find that they have much in common spiritually. They decide to meet and pray together. They have to agree on a time, place and manner in which to pray. If there is disagreement, how will they decide? Will one lead, and one follow? Is there a correct way, any guidelines?

Because there are people involved, the interpersonal aspects of humans relating to each other apply. If there are three or more, group dynamics come into play. If things are going to proceed in an orderly manner, structures and procedures are needed, whether or not they are written. It simply wouldn't work for a herd of people to enter a space on Sunday morning and begin to decide who's going to lead that day, and what they're going to do, and in which order. That assumes that they had agreed to come to the same place at the same time on Sunday morning. And who provided the space, and made sure it was unlocked, warm and clean?

Religion necessarily involves structure, rules and boundaries. What do we agree on? Who can be part of us? How do we figure out answers to questions? All of this external work can be done by people who each have a distinct loving relationship with God. It can also be done by people who don't have a personal relationship with God, but form a connection with a church. God is experienced in the liturgy, the rituals and beliefs of the church. Structure and predictability provide an opening. God may or may not be involved in the lives of individuals, but can be addressed in church.

Mysticism is a form of intense spirituality. It is inherently messy. The individual's life gets turned on its head. People wander, dazed. Some mutter incoherently (I have) others misunderstand and get lost on side paths. None of them are under anyone's control. How could they be? They claim to be guided by God. Can't get any higher than that. So who on earth can assert any authority over them? Or even want to keep them in their midst? No, far better that God stay on his side, and we'll stay on ours, everything safe and predictable.

Mysticism can be misused. Self-proclaimed prophets have led followers to a variety of bad ends. It's safer to reject all such claims, thus preserving the boundaries of established belief and practices.

Mysticism is a challenge to authority. Every Christian religion has evolved a source of truth, whether that be the Bible or religious leaders. I'm not aware of any group that encourages each individual to interpret the Bible entirely as they see fit. That could lead to the same chaos as mysticism. Rather, correct interpretation is usually left to a defined group of religious leaders. Tradition plays a part as well. "This is the way things should be done, because that is the way we've always done them."

Imagine someone standing up in church and saying, "God told me we should start an orphanage in Africa". Not, "I think we should start an orphanage, could someone direct me to the proper committee." By saying, "God told me", that person instantly took on a position of leadership, one that rivals whoever was leading. The choices for the group are few. Pressure that person to shut up (leave), or accept them as at least a new co-leader. In fact, if the group accepts the claim that "God told me", other leaders are in second place, unless they also had been accepted as God's spokesperson.

This situation would not go over well in most established churches. Leaders are to be respected and allowed to lead. New ideas should come from an appropriate source. Theology comes from Bishops or college theologians. Interpretations come from a minister or priest. New ideas for church enterprises typically come from church leaders, but may, if they follow protocol, rise from the membership. Religious truth does not come from a member saying, "God told me we should."

Unfortunately, and more painfully, an individual's personal experience can be rejected as well. It might seem that someone who reports, "God told me I should", would not be seen as a threat. After

24

all, they aren't telling anyone else what to do or believe. But this is a threat to the established order. How is the religious leader supposed to respond? Saying, "That's nice," seems to validate the statement. By claiming a direct connection, that individual gains status and power. Among atheists, they wouldn't; but among church people who presumably care about God, having the One talk directly to you yields instant status.

It also raises the specter of what's next? So, your present innocuous personal statement that God told you to take a vacation in Montana isn't a problem for anyone else. But what is God going to tell you next? We need to build a new church? Fire the minister? Move to Montana? No one knows.

"Why don't you keep that to yourself," would be the safer response. And that's what I've seen happen. Religious leaders and co-religionists have made it clear either subtly or clearly that they don't want to hear that stuff.

How sad. How devastating for the person who has had a strange, wonderful thing happen, but has nowhere to turn. Like a butterfly who sticks its head out of the cocoon in preparation for a glorious future, only to have someone turn out the lights. Lonesome, hungry, even desperate for understanding and companionship, they have nowhere to turn.

Many people do keep spiritual encounters to themselves. The more intense the experience, the more they may hide it, despite being so much in need of support. Of course, major internal shifts can't be completely hidden, and the individual will appear at times withdrawn, sad or radiant. Others may be attracted by the mysterious something the person is holding, and at other times repelled by the confusion and turmoil they display. I've watched ministers relate to congregants like this with a wary acceptance. True, the individual is sincere and involved in the church, but the minister can't ever be sure what they're going to do or say.

More frustrating to me is witnessing people deny or denigrate their own experiences. In doing so, they reject their own life and God's efforts to reach out to them.

The denials I've seen have usually occurred because God didn't connect in a way the person wanted or expected.

I've had someone tell me that they'd never had a direct experience of God. Later, the same person related how God spoke to them, but it didn't count, because it wasn't accompanied by a vision. They'd never seen heaven, or been fully in the presence of God, so they were still waiting for a genuine experience. I gently pointed out that how God shows up is not up to us, and that what had happened to them was a great blessing.

When listening to other's stories, I've heard people denigrate what they've known, saying in effect, "If it happened to me, it can't be important." One woman dismissed the profound condition of perpetually feeling the presence of God because she found it difficult to carry out daily Bible reading. Having been told that daily reading was a road to growth, she assumed her struggles with reading meant she hadn't grown very much spiritually. She concluded that feeling God's presence couldn't have much significance. I believe the daily readings were difficult because they weren't appropriate for her. In her humility, she had reversed what was happening.

This example is illustrative on several levels. She frustrated herself by expending resources on an ineffective spiritual practice. Self-blame created another obstacle. Failing to recognize the great gift she had received denied her the opportunity to understand and put it to use. It's like getting a wonderful birthday present and not opening it. Both she and the people around her didn't experience the benefits.

Now, it could be argued that God wanted the delay. Perhaps her frustrations were a necessary part of her learning. I have certainly seen in my own life that I may need a great deal of time to process.

So, does God only get involved in a few people's lives? Some select group, who may or may not realize what's happening? I've observed that the most common way God interacts in lives are 'serendipitous' happenings. They happen to many people but usually go unrecognized.

One evening, I drove to pick up my daughter at college so she could attend a political convention in our home town the next day. It was supper time, so we causally selected a restaurant. When driving there I make a poor decision and we were delayed for some time at a busy intersection. Had I turned left a block earlier, we would have saved at least ten minutes.

When we walked up to the counter to order, an older local Quaker couple I'd known for some time was pondering the menu. We decided to sit together. They shared that they'd never been to that restaurant, but had randomly decided to try it. At that point I smiled, recognizing that it wasn't an accident that we'd met at the counter just in time to decide to sit together. What God intended from our meeting wasn't clear, but there was no doubt in my mind that God had brought us together.

This wasn't the first time that God had used my mistakes to get me to the right place at the right time. The conversation shifted to political histories, and my daughter and I were fascinated by their stories of labor organizing long ago. On the way home, my daughter commented that those were the most liberal people she'd ever met. In her conversations with other students, she'd learned to mute her opinions after being razzed about being a radical. After meeting them, she felt more confident about standing her political ground the next day at the convention.

At that point I wasn't a safe driver, for my eyes filled with tears of gratitude for the blessings God had bestowed upon my daughter. To have brought 4 people across the city to that exact time and place so she could be reassured filled me with joy.

My daughter doesn't view the world in spiritual terms. When I gently shared my view of what we had experienced, she didn't see it. It was just interesting and helpful. We had sat side by side but came away with very different understandings of what had occurred.

This I believe is what happens all over, every day. Miracles take place and are ignored. Our attention is drawn to a beautiful flowering tree, and we are comforted. A friend calls at just the right time. Something bad happens that turns out for the best in the long run.

Those whose spiritual eyes have been opened, see. They have experienced enough of these instances and witnessed the effect they had on their interior life. They might have been the answer to prayers, or a call to action that began from a seemingly random event.

Those who have not had these experiences, don't accept that God was acting that directly. This last winter, I watched the ice form in a local river during weekly prayer walks. The current would force its way free during warmer weeks, only to have the ice close again after a cold spell. The state of the ice was one thing I noted and pondered each week as I sought out God in nature.

I looked forward to spring break up. This river has a history of spectacular ice jams under the right conditions. It warmed, and I was sure the ice would go. It held tight. I was afraid that I'd miss the event, for I was only at the park for a few hours a week.

I tried to schedule another walk, but was delayed. When I got to the park, the only ice left was a 500 feet long piece clinging to the south bank. I stood on the bridge looking, and suddenly realized that half of the piece was sliding under me. Silent, majestic, edges grinding and tipping, it crammed itself under the bridge and around the next bend.

I felt privileged to have seen this brief event and went on with my walk. Several hours later, I decided to cross the bridge one more time. Within moments, the last sheet of ice began to spin slowly and jammed itself part way under the bridge. Smaller pieces broke off the edges as the current flowed over and under this new obstacle.

On the way back to the car, I felt very blessed to have once again witnessed God working in the world – in this case, just to comfort me. It simply could not have been "luck" that these two events happened within moments of my climbing onto the bridge. The river hadn't been full of ice. This was the last of it.

"Whoa, wait a minute," you might be thinking. "Are you saying that God interfered with the laws of nature, just for your benefit?" That's not what I'm saying at all. Instead I'm saying something more wonderful – and frightening. God controlled me, without my knowledge.

A core belief for Quakers is that during our silent worship, God can speak to us. This occurs when someone feels moved to deliver a message. The task for those hearing the message is to determine whether what was said was meant for them, or perhaps for the group as a whole.

This seemingly straightforward scenario implies that God can control people's behavior. It's only a small step to say that I could be led to make a wrong turn and another couple could be led to a restaurant; or that my wanderings in a park could be timed by God so I arrived on a bridge just in time to see ice moving.

These last instances occurred without the individuals involved knowledge. It's as if people are God's marionettes, being moved about here and there to suit God's purposes. Moreover, it's being done without their permission.

What kind of world is this, if we're not in control of our own lives? From a mystical perspective, we never were. From conception to death, we live on this earth in the palm of God's hand. At times we make choices, and experience the consequences. In other instances, we follow God's hidden nudges to go here or there. One thing we can do is implore God, "Show me, teach me, guide me." Perhaps then we can sometimes glimpse God at work in our lives.

CONNECTIONS

Thus far, I've mentioned visions and voices. These have been my most common experiences, but others are known as well. This would be a good time to discuss ways people connect with God. Later, we'll talk about "spiritual gifts," phenomena that may occur as a result of being connected (like out of body experiences). But these gifts seem to me to be secondary. The core issue is the link with God.

People through history have reported having visions (both with eyes open and closed), hearing the voice of God or divine music, being touched by God, and divine smells.

It's interesting that these all use sensation as a way of approaching us. But that's no surprise, for this is how we take in all our information. I suppose God could use those flashes of intuition that occur unbidden in all of us that lead to new understandings. If I had huge new ideas suddenly occur to me I would either reject them, or worse yet claim them as entirely of my own making. Encountering God through sensation helps us realize this is "not I" but something outside of ourselves.

I have never encountered a divine aroma. Judging from what I've read, the experience is difficult to put into words. That's true of the rest of these phenomenon as well. What are important are elements from people's stories. Typically, they realize this is divine either at the time, or upon reflection. Something about the experience makes that clear. It evokes a powerful emotional response. It may bring a rapid understanding of complex concepts, and it tends to be memorable.

The experience itself is not as important as the emotional response or new understandings that result from it. After all, this process is not entertainment, but enlightenment and transformation. I've heard a number of people's descriptions of their epiphany experiences and am always struck by how mundane they are.

Someone will describe, with tears in their eyes and a trembling voice, how they were looking at a drop of dew on a leaf and were suddenly one with the universe. Their description leaves me unmoved, for it was so small, so ordinary. But what does move me is the rest of the story – the effect the experience had on them. The emotional impact is obvious. It may have been years ago, but was so memorable they can recall tiny details. The effect was so profound that despite having lasted only a few moments, it may have completely altered their life.

That's what our focus should be – what did they learn, how did they respond emotionally and where did it lead them. Non-mystics might tend to dwell on the experience itself, but they're only a means. That's like focusing on the timbre of someone's voice while ignoring what's being said.

It's not even the message itself that is important. If someone told me they received the message, "God loves you," it wouldn't invoke much of a response from me. If they went on and related how receiving that message had enabled them to take a step toward healing themselves that they hadn't conceived was possible, then they have my attention. For its the person's response to the event that allows us to judge not only it's validity (at least for them) but it's importance as well. We can then take it into ourselves, and see whether we can also learn from their experience.

So they saw a drop of dew on a leaf. If that were the end of the story, it wouldn't do anything for me. However, I never tire of hearing what happens next, especially when it was an initial epiphany experience. The stories of these spiritual infancies are enthralling.

Despite the preceding remarks about the relative unimportance of the events themselves, we need to spend some time describing what they may look like. If nothing else, it could serve to help your own experiences.

Seeing a drop of dew on a leaf and being opened is an example of having a vision with one's eyes open. I've had a number of people tell me this was their initial and peak experience of God. It's kind of strange when you think about it that something we do all day every day – looking at things – could be a portal to the Divine.

If you asked the person to describe what they saw, they may well have difficulty putting it into words. For me, inarticulate descriptions lend authenticity. Someone who blithely produces a polished account of what happened to them raises my suspicions, unless it happened many years ago. I know that I've spent years dwelling so much on my experience that I've rounded and smoothed and simplified it. For the first few years after it happened, I could barely stammer out two sentences about it.

But if they could describe having a vision with their eyes open, they would probably talk not of the object they were looking at, but of the world of the Spirit. For me, the trunks of trees have served as windows. On those few occasions when it's occurred, I've been looking at a tree, and become suddenly aware that I'm seeing through to the other side. My eyes continue to look at the tree, but my understanding is drawn somewhere else.

This is different from visually focusing on one thing, and shifting visual focus to something else. It's more like staring at something with unfocused eyes, with your mind not on what you're looking at. That's not an exact analogy, for I was visually focused on an object, which in turn pulled my attention somewhere else.

I know I stand stock still for the few minutes this occurs, overwhelmed internally but aware of my physical surroundings. It's not that the tree looks different, but I'm in effect looking through it. Perhaps it's because in processing the visual input that's occurring, I'm ascribing a much different meaning to what is happening.

Ecstasy is such a poor word to describe the emotional impact. It is just so marvelously wonderful to be caressed by God. To sample, however briefly, the boundless love that surrounds us.

Emotions may be all that occur, and are a life-sustaining blessing by themselves. Understanding may also be provided. Mystical insights have for me had two major components, awareness and meaning. Both of these occur very quickly, and are much broader than other mental processes.

If my eyes are open, clear visual images don't come to me. None the less, I can take in huge issues such as the need for forgiveness in one gulp. I may first observe the issue from a distance. Sometimes it feels that I'm standing far out in the universe, observing the human condition. Once I've taken in this new perspective, an accompanying understanding comes.

I may be called to a new task, or in the example of forgiveness be given more compassion because I better understand perpetrator and victim.

Always I am taught, nudged and lead to be more like God would like me to be; and caressed.

When visions occur during prayer with my eyes closed, the emotional element is the same, as is the process of awareness and understanding. The difference for me has been "seeing" sometimes vivid images as simple as a golden pencil, or as complex as glimpsing heaven or the universe. The visions seem to bring understanding more quickly, and act as powerful aids in remembering what was taught.

These visions are very brief. If timed, they would take only minutes. Their impact however can be profound.

I doubt that the contents of a vision would be very impressive to others. Sharing that I was given an understanding of the unimportance of race by "seeing" my fellow Quakers suddenly without any skin probably wouldn't impress you. It certainly struck me however. It was frankly horrible, seeing people I loved sitting across from me looking like they'd been under an anatomist's knife. It was a powerful message delivered in way that I've remembered clearly for over fifteen years.

I have heard the voice of God on only a few occasions. The messages provided very specific directions about specific issues. They weren't as vivid or memorable as the visions and didn't carry as much emotional content. That's perhaps because they lasted only as long as it takes to say a sentence or two.

You're probably wondering what God sounded like. Well, he/she sounded just like me. The messages came to me in the same internal language I think in.

In that case, how did I know it wasn't just me, thinking?

I can't tell you how I knew it was God and not me. But, there was no doubt. They were coming from outside me. There was one time I questioned whether it was God or me.

I was at work at the end of the day straightening things up when I got the message, "Go see Molly." (I've changed the name.) I'd never gotten a message from God while at work, wasn't feeling prayerful, and wasn't aware of any reason I should go see Molly; so I continued to putter around my office. I decided to wait, open to whatever would happen. Moments later, the message was repeated, "Go see Molly," in the same manner as before. I stopped what I was doing and went to see her, convinced now that it was indeed God who was talking to me.

Molly had some mental health issues, and was going through a difficult time at work. We talked for some time, and I was able to reassure and support her. I walked away afterward, marveling at how much God loved Molly. Looking back years later, I continue to be comforted by the thought that God could make use of me. I'm also struck by how much he/she was protecting this woman, perhaps because her mental illness increased her needs.

Touch is another kind of connection spoken of less often then visions or voices. I remember one instance when I was praying, earnestly seeking comfort. I felt my shoulder being "touched" even though I was alone at the time. It kind of startled me, but I recognized it as God's touch. Very gentle, but there.

The other occasion was more complex. During a retreat, I went to the chapel late at night. I sat on a bench to pray and after a while was moved to kneel on the floor, something I never do. After a short time, I felt God's arms encircle me. Nothing dramatic; I was simply being tenderly held. I had a sense that this was God as companion. In the ensuing days, when I closed my eyes and stilled I could feel that embrace. I knew I wasn't alone, couldn't be alone, for God was with me.

That touch has continued to this day, over ten years later. You'd think after receiving that kind of blessing I'd be patient, kind, generous and display all the other fruits of the Spirit. But no, I'm impatient, selfish, sad and so on and so forth on a regular basis. When I stop wallowing in my flawed humanness for a moment; close my eyes and still, those arms are there. My Divine Companion.

These are fairly intense experiences. I experience visions and hear the voice of God only occasionally. They have not occurred as answers to specific questions. One time that I can remember getting a direct answer was in response to my earnest plea, "Tell me which is the better choice," and got the answer, "That's what I gave you brains for."

Frequently, I don't get answers, and I am left to figure it out for myself. There are two approaches to discerning the will of God. One is to do nothing unless God says "Yes". In Quaker history, I've heard this termed the "quietest" approach. The opposite, activist approach would be to move ahead with what seems best, unless God says, "No". At different times, I've used both.

Both methods depend upon a feeling I get, a deep sense that I am in harmony with God. It's not a clear answer, but it allows me to continue. I believe that all people, if they seek God's will, can experience this harmony. They may never have an intense experience, but can live a Spirit-led life. The other ingredient necessary, in addition to seeking God's will, is a willingness to listen to what God wants. We may not like what we hear, but communication can only take place if we listen.

I've used the quietest approach when the situation is very confusing; when I am the only one involved in the outcome; when there is no time limit; when inaction will not result in harm. The further I walk on this journey, the more I've come to value the act of surrendering to God's will. This passive approach doesn't come naturally to me, but has become very sweet. God rarely seems to be in a rush.

When rigidly applied as the only approach one uses, quietism can become an excuse for inaction. We need to discern how to discern.

The activist approach has a lot of appeal, for it mimics contemporary society. "Get it done, make things happen," are common themes for us, both at work and in our home lives. It certainly is much faster to tell God, "I'm going to do this, unless you tell me right now not to." If we don't hear anything within a few minutes, we are ready to proceed. I'm not silly enough to insist that God answer me right now, but I have moved on issues after only a day or two of waiting. This approach seemed most appropriate when the "right" thing to do was fairly clear; when inaction could result in harm; when I was acting unselfishly; when my efforts would be largely anonymous. These last two factors helped reduce the influence my self-interest and ego might play in the decision. (Darn it, I can't say that God wants me to eat that candy bar.)

Sometimes, I'm simply confused, and don't know what to do. Should I go ahead without an answer? What if the question is not to act, but instead is whether to choose this or that? When time permits,

I simply wait, while I attempt to stay open to the Spirit's leading. If I haven't felt a nudge in either direction and it's time to decide, then I have to trust. Trust that God is working in my life, and that I have learned enough to keep my feet on the path.

In the end, all will be well. What seems a disaster now will probably bear fruit that I might not perceive until well afterwards. But all things, including time, return to God. Trust has been a central issue in my spiritual life. Learning to trust God, and later learning to trust myself.

The biggest frustrations I'm aware of in the realm of spirituality arise in people who have developed a sense of living in harmony with God, but desire more intense experiences. All I can offer is the observation that intense experiences occur because God wills it and the individual is open to receive what is given. How can we develop our receptivity? The best way I know is daily prayer which includes large doses not only of talking to God, but of listening.

My intense experiences came unbidden and undeserved. I hope spiritual people never get into a "mine's bigger or better" contest about what they've encountered on their paths. These examples are offered to reassure readers that they are not alone and to offer support in climbing that hill or taking that next leap of faith. I have been blessed. Wonderfully, greatly blessed. My prayer is that others may be as well.

MY SPIRITUAL JOURNEY

Having talked about what we're talking about, it's time for me to provide my own background. Not because I think it's wonderful or special, but to serve as a way to illustrate a number of issues. What happened to me is an example of what this book is about – mystical experiences happening today in a western culture.

I was physically and emotionally abused throughout my childhood by my mother, who died several years ago. We'll talk later about why the gender of my abuser is important. If I displayed any anger about my treatment I was beaten more, so I learned to withdraw emotionally. Added to a native shyness, I came to feel most comfortable alone. When faced with conflict, to this day I am quick to withdraw. Physically if I can, emotionally in any case.

I was raised Protestant by proximity. My parents sent us kids to the nearest Protestant church, changing denominations as we moved several times. Neither of my parents attended church. Looking back, I see that Sunday mornings were the only time they had the house to themselves. We spent most of our youth in the United Church of Christ just down the road. I learned about the Bible and current religious issues. When I was 15, I decided I was an atheist. I don't remember what led up to that conclusion. Part of it may have been that I didn't like having to listen to sermons. As young as I was, I sometimes found that I had thought more deeply about a sermon's subject than the minister.

Camping, fishing and canoeing were my main hobbies as a child. While (stupidly) canoeing on a flooded river early in the spring when I was 16, we collided with some debris and tipped over. I ended up draped over a half-submerged log, the strong current dragging at my rubber boots. I knew that if my boots pulled me under, I was likely to hit my head on the log, or get tangled in the branches underwater. I'd probably drown.

I surprised myself by praying for help. I managed to crawl on top of the log, where another canoe was able to stop and pull me off. On the drive home, I thought about having prayed. If I was going to be honest with myself, I had to admit that I was not an atheist. I went looking for the truth – someone who could tell me about God with a great deal of authority.

I found Catholicism. To this day, I love Catholic liturgy. The music, language and even the smells speak deeply to me. I attended confirmation classes and was ready to be baptized. My mother refused permission. My father was raised Catholic, my mother Protestant. When they went to his priest to get married, the rule was that she either had to convert, or they both had to sign a paper that they would raise their children Catholic. For whatever reason, they were both offended by this and got married by a justice of the peace. My mother harbored a resentment against the Catholic Church.

Living at home while going to college, I became so desperate to leave that I enlisted in the Army when I was 19, at the height of the Vietnam War build up. A counselor later characterized this as akin to a suicide attempt. Fortunately for me, I was sent to Germany. I no longer needed permission to become a Catholic, and was baptized and confirmed.

When the opportunity arose, I became a Catholic chaplain's assistant. This meant serving mass daily with an American priest. The American traveled on the weekends to outlying bases, and a German priest served mass on Sundays. The German priest was witty and sociable, and enjoyed sharing gossip about the workings of the church in Rome.

I was content as a Catholic. I recognized that I had too strong a sex drive and was too rebellious to be a candidate for the priesthood, but I was very devout. After several years, the Humanie Vitae encyclical was published, prohibiting birth control. I was opposed to it, but willing to accept it as an example of the Church calling members to a high standard of conduct.

The German priest was incensed and shared the process that led up to the decision. He described it as a combination of politics and personality. I was shocked, for I'd come to Catholicism because the Church proclaims itself as the arbiter of truth. When the Pope speaks, what comes out of his mouth is what God wants for the modern world. I'd assumed some kind of direct connection between the Pope and God. Now, I was told that truth was being derived by what sounded like a flawed human process.

I lost my faith in the Church. Fortunately, this occurred shortly before I was discharged from the Army, for I increasingly had difficulty serving Mass. I came home unchurched, and remained that way for about twenty years. I continued to believe in God, but had no desire to participate in an organized religion.

I went to college, and 'just happened' to find my way into a profession that helped me in a number of ways. I find it very difficult to learn foreign languages. Because of all the other required course work, an Occupational Therapy degree didn't require a foreign language. So, I chose it as a stepping stone to becoming a psychologist (which I ended up not pursuing). The knowledge I gained in studying and practicing as an Occupational Therapist gave me a deep knowledge of neuropsychology, and why my sensory system was so hypersensitive. Several therapists helped me heal.

I married just after college and discovered that a dysfunctional childhood is not a good preparation for a blissful marriage. We stayed and grew together, but it hasn't been easy. I was aware that the baggage I was carrying interfered with my ability to relate completely to my wife, and that there were skills I lacked. I wasn't sure what to do with the baggage, and wasn't sure what those skills were.

My first professional job was in a state hospital, serving patients with chronic mental illness. Many of them had been in for decades. Some had survived the era of lobotomies and frequent shock treatments. Some were angry, some apathetic, but happiness was noticeably absent. Their lost, shattered lives continue to haunt me.

We adopted two babies from Korea, several years apart. I waited until I was nearly forty and had a chance to watch several of my siblings raise children. Deathly afraid that I was caught in the victim/victimizer cycle, I hadn't trusted myself to be a parent. When I saw that my siblings weren't abusive, I came to trust that I could be a good father.

Parenting those little ones was the happiest period of my life. I had never known unconditional love, and reveled in it. For eight years, I worked half time so I could spend more time at home with them.

When the oldest child entered school, we decided that it was time to find a Sunday school for her. I still didn't want to be lectured to, so Protestant churches were out. I'd recently read Mitchner's

Chesapeake, and his description of a carpenter building a meeting house had touched me. With this renewed awareness of Quakerism, I attended a Meeting and immediately felt at home. I began to search for a connection to God, using imagery I'd learned in whole-body therapy. Slowly, I made progress.

I came to revere a mature couple in the Quaker Meeting. There were spiritually seasoned and I came to think of them as spiritual parents. The woman was seriously injured in a car accident. It was suspected at first that she would be totally paralyzed.

I was devastated. A life time's worth of pain, compiled from my childhood and the lives of my patients added to my flood of feelings. I felt that I was at the bottom of a deep well. During silent worship the next Sunday, I internally screamed at God, "How could you let this happen to such a loving, spiritual, good person. I demand an answer!"

In response, I was lifted to heaven, and was fully in the presence of God for about 10 minutes by the clock. This was my epiphany, the only time I've been so immersed in heaven. I walked away with only two initial truths - that heaven is forever, and

God is perfect love. I've been processing that ten minutes for the last twenty years. It became the touch stone of my life.

Now, I suspect you're thinking, "Whoa, wait a minute. Let's go into this a little more." And you're right. There are many aspects to talk about (assuming you're still willing to entertain that I'm telling the truth).

For a start, every time I hear a religious leader say, "We can't know what heaven is like," I think, "Wait a minute, I was there!" But I immediately realize they probably don't want to hear what I have to say. For that is my truth. I did see heaven, and I do know God exists. No question. No doubt. That's my reality, and I now go on from there.

So, what is heaven like? Overwhelming! I remember a royal purple sky with stars, and being surprised by the plasticity of time and space, as well as glimpsing that they were interchangeable. I sensed the presence of many souls, but immediately was consumed by the presence of the One. I felt as if all the love of every mother throughout the world, and throughout time, was given to me. I was surrounded, permeated, suffused, saturated with

God's love for me. Nothing else mattered. Nothing else could matter in the face of such love. The huge love that was given to me in no way diminished the love given to every other soul.

Heaven for me is thus very simply being swallowed up by Perfect Love. I've come to understand a few aspects such as how we relate to the souls of people we've lived with, and to the histories of our behavior while we were on earth, but these are minor elements when compared to the central reality of God's tremendous love.

What bliss. An infant's face lights up and their eyes stare in wonder at their mother's smiling face. So shall we, when we encounter God. Everything else fades into the background. To be so loved. So tremendously wonderfully loved. Forever.

This is what awaits us on the other side.

There are a number of other questions you might have. Who gets to go to heaven? What about being judged? Who will I meet there? In this case, someone else's suffering was the catalyst. What's up with that? Let's leave these questions for later, so the chronology of this story can continue. We'll get back to each of those questions.

So, what was the answer I got to the question I screamed at God? Why did this dear friend have to suffer?

I learned the perspective of heaven. Forever is a difficult concept for me to fully grasp. Sure, the definition is simple. When I was in heaven, I experienced it. Bliss. Never ending. Tender, nurturing personal love for me that went on and on and on.

This world is a wonderful, terrible place where very good, and very bad things happen. But this life is so fleeting. Heaven is forever. This was a fundamental, wrenching adjustment to my world view. I had lived centered on the world around me. Now, I needed to learn to live a heaven centered life.

But first, I have to figure out what had happened to me. Had I gone crazy? Imagined this – made it up in my own head? What did it mean? What should I do about it?

I had no words, no context. For six months, I told no one what had happened

DANCE

I could want nothing more
than to dance in the palm of God.

Surrounded by Friends
whose tender concern
lifts me.

To go forth in Love-lit mist
seeing dimly, but forever.

My ear turned
inward

outward

and I know
and knowing leap yes!
Yes.

Dazed by the touch of forgiveness
I wander through the world.

God was very tender with me. Whenever my awareness wasn't being pulled somewhere by people or tasks I looked inward, and there she was – Holy Spirit Mother. Comforting me with her presence. One of the places at work that my attention wasn't demanded by others was in the bathroom. At first, I rejected my own experience of encountering Holy Spirit Mother in the bathroom as being unworthy, inappropriate. With time, I smiled inwardly at this new definition of a prayer stall. Strange, vulgar, but a powerful example of how God loved me totally, just as I was.

Scared, confused and filled with joy, my mind was preoccupied with attempting to understand. By 'accident' I found a book on mysticism by Evelyn Underhill. Now, I at least had a word for what I was experiencing. I could tell that she had experienced something similar, but the emphasis in this particular book didn't speak to me. She spoke of the importance of mystics, frightening me. I was just a confused, weak individual.

Externally, I probably appeared even less outgoing than usual. The woman whose accident occasioned my epiphany slowly healed, eventually making a full recovery. During Sunday worship, I felt deeply connected to Holy Spirit Mother, and experienced a number of brief visions that taught and guided me.

Slowly, I learned to view life from the perspective of heaven. The transitory nature of our time here was reinforced. I came to see that outcomes were less important than efforts. The means is the end, for if I could do the smallest thing with great love, I would be living as I should.

After about six months I decided to apply for membership in my local Quaker Meeting. This would include meeting with a small group and sharing my spiritual journey. I had not heard any of them speak of spiritual experiences in ways similar to mine. I was afraid that they would reject me once they found out what was going on inside me, not wanting such a weirdo in their midst.

My experiences were more intense and messier than what they were used to, but they warmly accepted me. I was very relieved, and no longer felt so alone.

About this time, I shared what I'd experienced with my wife. She was nonplussed to discover that our marriage had become a threesome, and it took some time for her to adjust to the idea. I'll speak more about the effect of spiritual events on human relationships later.

For the next year, I often had visions while worshiping in Meeting on Sundays. Some were wonderfully comforting. In response to my pleading for reassurance, I "saw" Holy Spirit Mother cover me with a blanket. From this vision, I developed my nickname for God – Sweet Comforter.

Others were jarring and frightening. While contemplating about racism, I "saw" how God views our external selves by glimpsing the people surrounding me without any skin. I had done cadaver dissection in college, and to see people I loved in this condition was horrifying. It was memorable however, which I think was God's purpose. It also taught me about how little importance God places on what we humans put so much effort and pride into – our appearance.

I found that I often wanted to be outdoors. Somehow, I felt closer to God there. Moonlight felt very comforting. I seemed to be able to feel it falling on me and in turn pulling me out of myself to connect with the One.

I signed up for a program that included two retreats and the formation of small groups that would meet and share about our spiritual lives. These Quaker retreats were held in a beautiful Catholic center. The first evening, I went out fairly late and sat under some apple trees to pray. I noticed that Holy Spirit Mother didn't come to me. When I reflected on it, I realized that she hadn't been with me for some weeks.

That may sound strange, but I guess I was so used to her that I took her presence for granted. Now that I was at a retreat I wanted to hang out with her for an extended period, rather than brief encounters during my busy life. I was upset and confused about her absence as I went in to bed.

I went about our activities during the next day. Late that night, I got up and went to the chapel to pray. It was a large chapel, with high windows that faced south. Moonlight streamed in and fell on the floor in front of the altar, so that's where I went to sit. I prayed for understanding, pleading for Holy Spirit Mother to come to me. In response, I "saw" myself as a kindergartner, standing on the back steps of my home, pounding to be let in. It was the first day of school and time for me to let loose of mom's apron strings and toddle off on my own.

I was bereft, and sat weeping and rocking for a long time. As the moonlight moved across the floor, I moved with it. God blessed me by giving me the understanding that this was not a punishment, but simply a part of growing. As I gradually calmed and opened myself, I became aware that there was a force flowing out of my palms. "What is this?" I asked, and came to understand that it was the power of the Holy Spirit. "What do you want me to do with it?" I asked, and was told that it was a great gift, that I must care for and never misuse.

To this day, I haven't been given specific uses for this gift, but it did serve as a powerful reassurance that God hadn't abandoned me. No one had even hinted that my relationship with God would change. I hadn't thought about it, but didn't realize either that God was in charge, not me. I still kick myself for having taken the presence of Holy Spirit Mother for granted those months. If only I'd known that this precious gift would be mine for such a short time. But I guess it makes sense. Babies take their mothers for granted, and she was with me when I was a spiritual infant.

The past fifteen years have been a period of slow growth. Does anyone manage to mature spiritually? What does that mean? I'm not sure, but over the years I came to grips with a number of issues. I did manage with a lot of God's help to keep going, but I'm also very aware that I'll never get it right.

My observation has been that each person has different long-term issues given to them to wrestle with. Pain, anxiety, trust, forgiveness, illness (physical or mental), loss, abundance, desire each make separate demands. Whether planted by nature or nurture, their pull to this earth act as spiritual restraints. Perhaps saints can banish their issues. I certainly can't. But the spiritual life lies partly in the struggle itself. Falling down and having to get back up, over and over. Taking a step forward, only to see you've taken a step back.

Some of my issues included trust and desires to be nurtured and respected. They served as canvases for God to present me with challenges. I seemed to face things one at a time, usually for months. Some I overcame after repeated failures. Others I finally came to realize I couldn't handle, and had to beg God to rescue me.

Irony and paradox, pain and ecstasy, satisfaction and failure have been constants. I've come to accept that my spiritual life will continually change. I have a great deal to learn, and learning is hard.

The next chapters will discuss themes, challenges and issues I encountered, and share what I gathered from them.

RECOVERING FROM AN EPIPHANY

For nearly six months after my peak experience, I told no one what I'd experienced. My thoughts and emotions were in a turmoil. I kept wondering what had happened, for I hadn't heard or read of anything like this. Was I going crazy? What would happen next? What was I supposed to do? What would others think?

Beneath these fears was a deep joy, wonder and awe. Once or twice, I questioned whether I had really been in heaven with God. But each time I thought back to those ten minutes, I recognized that what I'd seen and felt was true, more real and more certain than my three dimensional surroundings.

I felt so blessed and grateful. My fears were eased by a presence I came to know as Holy Spirit Mother. Each time I stilled, she was there, consoling and reassuring me. Despite having had my life instantly turned upside down, I didn't have to worry about what was going to happen next. I wasn't going crazy. All would be well.

I wasn't exactly praying, but I was constantly looking inward trying to understand and process. I began to reexamine my beliefs and understandings. Sometimes it felt like I was standing in heaven and looking down at the world. From that perspective, things looked quite different and I had much to learn. I kept coming back to the proposition, "If God is perfect love, then how would God feel about...."

One of the first things I understood is that God isn't concerned about what gender each member of a couple is, but is concerned about the quality of their relationship. Are they loving, faithful, supportive and unselfish with each other? Sadly, I saw that they often aren't, whether straight or gay.

I continued to worship with Quakers, and often had visions during our silent worship. These lasted only a few minutes, but each served to instruct me. The visual images helped fix the accompanying understanding in my mind. They also reassured me that I was still connected to God. The whole thing wasn't a fluke. Things would turn out OK because I was being helped.

As I continued to have visions and learned more, I felt different, very different. I recognized that I had received a great blessing. Thank goodness I was given enough wisdom and strength, for I nearly

67

became lost. Something special had happened that transformed me. I felt so much bigger, deeper, better than I had been. Didn't that make me special? Even though my flaws were being clearly illuminated, wasn't I something different, set apart from others?

I've been a blood donor for a long time. I remember watching the blood flow out of me and thinking, "Someone will get the blood of a mystic. I wonder if that will do something special for them?"

I kept thinking that I should do something wonderful with the gifts I'd been given. Now that I was so different, surely I could do great things. This misunderstanding that I had been transformed and was therefore special, and desire to accomplish great tasks were one of the greatest temptations I ever faced. Focusing on my specialness was also a huge distraction from the real work I should have been doing – learning obedience and humility.

This is how monstrous spiritual leaders can be born. Intoxicated by the changes they see in themselves, and convinced they know more than mere mortals, they can charge off in any direction. The attraction some followers feel for a leader who is spiritually connected provides opportunities for tragedy.

About that time, God called me back to reality. I went through a period of being shown God's glory, alternated with being presented with my faults. My vision was pulled back and forth between these extremes for days. It was agonizing to see God's perfection juxtaposed with my limitations, lusts and unworthiness. Finally, I was driving to a retreat and felt so awful I had to pull over in a small park. I sat there and began praying aloud, "God, please take this away. I can't stand the pain. I know I am nothing. Will always be nothing. Please Lord, lift this from me."

After some more prayer, I drove on. I remember that lesson in humility to this day. In a later vision I saw that I was a damaged, flawed clay pot. God touched me, and I became more like God wished, but remained damaged and flawed. And so I will always remain. I often wonder why God came to someone so unworthy.

Along with obedience, humility has been one of my life long tasks. It has also kept me out of trouble. How horrible – and dangerous – it would be for me to go about thinking that I have the answers and should be granted this or that role or privilege. Far better that I was taught that I am one of the least, where I can rest safely in the arms of Love.

When I came out of my spiritual closet after six months, I was pleasantly surprised. My fellow Quakers were accepting, telling me that Quakerism is a mystical religion. The intensity of my experiences were unusual but within that tradition. I was surprised as well that my extended family had realized on some level what had happened to me, without my having said a word. Somehow, it was obvious in my appearance and behavior.

I still had great difficulty articulating – or even comprehending – what was going on. Writing poems helped me process, but I couldn't form coherent sentences about my interior life. It was too overwhelming, and stayed that way until now – twenty years later.

I have had a few people accept my statement that I was a mystic who then assumed that I must be some wonderfully accomplished perfectly self-controlled guru. I quickly point out that when God starts with a flawed vessel, the end result remains flawed. Spiritual lessons can't be learned in a lifetime and I will never overcome my animal self. I've been given no special powers, no ability to heal the circumstances of others. I've become a devoted student and servant. Nothing more.

GIFTS verses CONCLUSIONS

We need to make an important distinction here between what a mystic is told and sees during contacts with the Divine, and conclusions they draw based on their experiences. If listeners should take a mystic's reports of visions and voices with a grain of salt, they should evaluate conclusions they draw from their experiences with two grains.

When I had my vision of fellow Quakers without any skin, I was given an understanding that while our appearance is important to us, it isn't important from the perspective of heaven. The jarring vision increased the emotional impact and seared the lesson into my memory. This was the case with many visions. What I saw helped me take in and remember an accompanying understanding.

I pondered the lesson I had been given in that vision for years, and came to further understand that God values each third world person, no matter how poor, exactly the same way She values me. Despite the immensely greater wealth, opportunity, education and possessions I have, God cares equally about each human life. A sense of obligation to share with those who have less grew, and I went on to develop other understandings.

The original vision included knowledge given to me. I didn't have to link one idea with another. I was given an understanding. Others might reject my report, but my only part was reporting what appeared to me as facts – we are all equal in God's eyes, our outward appearances matter little in God's eyes.

My concerns for the poor in third world countries were outgrowths of the original vision. They involved my thought processes, taking the original ideas and applying them. These conclusions were influenced by my knowledge, comprehension and values and therefore are more colored by who I am.

Thus, the content of visions and voices reveals more of God, and less of the mystic, then subsequent conclusions. Of course, the personality of the mystic does influence the original visions. We'll talk more in the following chapters about ways God chooses to appear, and the different ways mystics pay attention.

It's relatively easy for listeners to evaluate a mystic's report, "God said ......". The mystic is either providing an accurate report, or they're not. When they go on to say, "And this leads me to believe that.....," we have to take the mystic's limitations and personal history into account.

Please note the language differences between, "God told me...," and "Therefore I believe that..." The former is a report. The latter places the speaker in much the same position as the rest of humanity, relying on their own understandings and what they believe to shape new notions.

I will endeavor here to let you know which realm we are dealing in, so you know how much salt to use. The first portion of this book will deal with the mystical process, and reports of what I saw and heard. At the end, I will share the products of years of pondering what I've experienced. Mysticism is in many ways timeless and universal. The fruits that mystics germinate within themselves are more specific, speaking to issues in a particular culture at a particular point in time.

IRONY AND PARADOX

Having cautioned about being analytical, I now invite you not to do so. We won't get very far spiritually if we confine ourselves to the world of the intellect. But what else is there? Isn't it an invitation to madness if we supplant rational thinking?

Later, we'll need to discuss differences between mental illness and mysticism, but I'm suggesting that there is a knowing that goes beyond the mind. Having said that, I'll back up a step and assert that our spiritual experiences shouldn't violate our knowledge.

Creationism, with it's belief that the world was formed 10,000 years ago – replete with sedimentary rocks, buried dinosaur bones, DNA traces back in time and so forth – appears to me to violate the tenets of every branch of science. Believing it would require me to turn my brain off. This I refuse to do.

I may have mystical experiences that startle or even frighten me. They may radically alter my understanding, and may even be incomprehensible. At no time has God ever asked me to be stupid.

Instead, I've been required to wrestle for understanding with every faculty I have, for years if need be.

Not too long after my opening, I was walking in a park. The following poem came to be.

ALL OF ME

Come.
Come on, come on, come on, come on.

I would gather you under my arms;
good and evil,
life and death,
love and hatred.

I love thee,

I am thee.

When I looked at what I had written, I was shocked. It was easy to accept that I am all those things. But how in the world could I say I loved evil and hatred?

I didn't reject what I'd written, but looked hard to see where it had come from. Was this my unconscious? Had I just been 'creative' or flip? When I took those questions into prayer, earnestly seeking understanding, it was clear that this had come from God. I not only didn't understand, but was horrified at the thought. None the less, I took this gift, tucked it deep inside me and resolved to work on it.

Part of my spiritual work has been to struggle with my faults. Over a period of years, I finally learned that I must stop denying things I don't like about myself. The first step in dealing with them is to face them. The next step, that took more years to learn, is to embrace them. Yes, I am selfish, lustful, jealous and on and on. Denying, pushing away and suppressing all took energy. When I did this, I kept myself under control but remained full of faults.

When I acknowledged faults and accepted that they were part of me, I gained control over them. They were not to be feared, but loved. I am a human, made as God constructed me. Limited, flawed, damaged; and dearly beloved by God, just as I am. If I am to grow in love for others and for God, I must learn to love myself. A first step is acknowledging who I am.

During the years I was working to learn a process to accept who I am, I kept thinking back to the poem. Would my thoughts encompass what it implied? Not yet? Well then, let's get back and dig deeper.

To get back to my point, God never demanded that I violate my intelligence. I was expected to observe, learn and think. The process expands my horizons and broadens my understanding. I question more, not less.

Trust has been an issue for me, trusting God, and trusting that I will respond adequately. I've come to completely trust that God won't give me more than I can handle and will never lead me astray. Into some strange places, yes. But as long as it is God handing me the issues, I can throw myself into learning and growing in love.

I think I would only get into trouble if I surrendered my intellect to someone else. I obey God. I surrender to God. I welcome the incomprehensible from God and make it a part of me until I do comprehend. All this is safe, for it is between God and me. I welcome other's observations and conclusions, but am obliged to run them through my own discernment. That discernment must include laying questions before God in humility and patience. It also includes thinking as deeply as I can, and making use of whatever knowledge I can gather.

Much of my learning takes place by looking backward. So often, it's what happens afterwards that givens meaning to the things happening right in front of us. The irony and paradox become apparent.

I try something I believe God wants me to do, and fail. Although I feel terrible at the time, six months later I see the good that resulted. I surrender, feeling weak and helpless in this fierce world, and become more effective. I begin a task, certain that I understand its purpose, only to see later that a resulting casual conversation was perhaps the most important thing that occurred.

I'm confused and completely uncertain about what will happen as I go about God's work. And that's fine, for if I'm to allow the Spirit to work though me, I can't be in control. It's frightening. Demeaning too. I'm supposed to be a competent adult. Here I am often passive, habitually weak and uncertain. Apparently just the way God wants me.

All those years of witnessing irony and paradox have led to this. What a strange way to learn.

What a strange thing to do – surrendering not just my will, but my competence and any sense of control.

How wonderful to rest, content, in the arms of God.

But what of this knowing that began this discussion. It's true that I do use my intelligence, my rational thought, to comprehend what's going on, even if it's in the rear view mirror. Where's the non-rational thinking come in?

Rather than calling it irrational, I prefer to think that there is a transcendent way of knowing- the knowledge of the soul.

FUNCTIONS OF THE SOUL

Science has expanded our knowledge, from the ocean depths to the outer reaches of the universe, ever deeper into the atom and back in time. One area of the human experience that remains unknown is the soul. That's odd, for we all have one. Moreover, it forms our very core and is the center of our existence. The base of our memory, love, wisdom and personhood. A container for a divine spark or blinding light.

Yet many deny its existence. Most ignore its presence. Let's take some functions one by one.

Memory. I have been trained in Cranio-Sacral therapy, an alternative treatment that works well for releasing repressed trauma. It involves therapists laying their hands over the sites of old injuries. I witnessed clients dredge up memories from infancy, from before they had language or clear understandings. Not just my ears, my hands told me they were reporting accurately. Where had they stored these memories? In their soul.

This may be part of what abuse survivors mean when they speak of having damaged souls. Not just their physical and emotional selves have been hurt. Below that, a sense of unworthiness may lead to a belief that they are no longer able to connect with God. They believe they're so damaged that God wants nothing to do with them.

Nothing could be further from the truth.

If they could but see it, God is bending over them, weeping. If only they would turn, fling their arms up and cry, "Come to me, for I'm broken. I give up and I'm ready to listen." For the barrier is very thin between the hopeless and the Divine.

Our souls can not be sullied or damaged by others. Filled with painful memories, yes. More painful still when we add our measure of guilt and shame.

If only there was someone, some place or way for people to take in and truly hear the message, "God loves you." I have often thought it would make an ideal theme for a weekend retreat for participants to be told, "God loves you. Just as you are. Right now, right here." Over and over again, in as many ways as possible, with time in between to absorb the message.

Love. Human love, even at its best, contains an element of self.

"I love this rose with its delicate petals, tinted so subtly." (This rose pleases me. In several days, it won't engender these feelings in me, and I won't like it anymore.)

"I love this person because of the way they act toward me, and the tender feelings their presence evokes." (If someday I don't like how they behave, or if my feelings diminish, so will my love for them.)

There are those who are instinctively giving. Helping others is a basis of their identity, their worth. While accomplishing great things, their efforts typically are sustained by seeing positive results.

While laudable, there is another level of loving, one that embraces holy foolishness. When judged strictly on a human level, selfless love is not in the best interest of the individual. The assistance that goes unnoticed, the anonymous donation (with no tax deduction or other benefit) makes no sense.

To take the hand of the dying, when they might not even be aware of your presence, to give to those who sneer at your motives seem silly. Caring about those who suffer in far off countries, when you will never see them and can do little for them. Giving up your life, not in some quick glorious death, but living every day doing things you'd prefer not to.

Ultimately, dying to yourself and to this world. For what? For a God who can't be seen, or touched with human hands.

Only the soul can carry this unselfish love and sustain it.

Wisdom. Different from knowing, wisdom implies good judgment. The deepest wisdom comes from seeing widely and deeply through the eyes of love. This is the basis for the Eastern tradition of the 'third eye' and the western phrase 'eyes of the soul'. For we can see with our soul.

One of the common metaphors for an epiphany experience is being 'opened'. Early on, I had many visions of being lifted out of myself and way into the cosmos, then looking down on the human condition. This new way of seeing caused me to rethink all that I had assumed.

Now, I try to go about the world with my spiritual eyes open, looking for God in all that I see. This looking involves all of me – taking in, thinking, loving, praying. I am open, present with, available. I have to add the caveat that I also sometimes go about with my spiritual eyes closed, self-absorbed and whining, being grumpy, angry and so on.

Seeing widely for the mystic also means being shown that we are all one, living in the heart of God. Wrestling with this truth until it becomes instinctive and we know fully and deeply that there is no "us and them", there is not even a "me and not me". The person I am looking at, the person I am hearing about, is me. I am starving, ill, being abused, exploited. I am suffering and dying. Being ignored and rejected. That stinking, shambling homeless person I stepped around is me.

Seeing deeply means looking into people's souls, to find God. In those who disagree, dislike, harm me. Greeting that God. Taking a long view of issues, acknowledging my own blindness, and God's infinite mercy, painted across an infinity of time.

All will be well. All must be well, for all things return to a merciful, loving God, to dwell in love for eternity.

This love – huge, blessed, miraculous love, is so large it can only be held in our souls.

Personhood. Our soul is the part of us that is eternal. Our physical self, which we take so much pride in/are ashamed of and has given us great joy/pain drops away. Any intellectual knowledge/skills we possess will be overwhelmed when our eyes are fully opened in heaven. Across time and around the world, people believed that death is not the end. Whether through rebirth or as spirits/ghosts, they would live on.

When I was eighteen, I enlisted in the Army during the Vietnam War. Basic training was brutal, designed to instill compliance through fear. The guys who were older when they were drafted retained their personalities and sense of self. Those of us who were younger were cowed into submission. I was fortunate enough to be sent to Germany. After about six months, I noticed that "I" had returned. Freed from fear I was myself again, a sentient being once more.

Where had "me" gone during the time I was broken? To my core, the deepest part of me. I retreated to my soul. We can be beaten, broken and defeated; forced by circumstances to do things we wouldn't otherwise countenance. We retain our soul, and our soul continues to hold a spark of the Divine. God held our souls before we were born, and we retain that touch in this life. We are not divine. The gift of God's love we carry through this life is.

Every human life is sacred. We reflect God's glory and are the canvas upon which that glory can be made manifest.

Not only can those outside us not extinguish this spark, neither can we. A lifetime dominated by poor choices – drug abuse, prostitution and violence may bury that spark, but it continues to burn. No one is beyond redemption, no one is worthless despite whatever they have done. All of us can, at any time, merely turn our face to the Light. God's breath will begin to grow that spark into a roaring conflagration that, if we allow it, will consume our lives with love.

GOD IS NOT A TALKING PURPLE FIRE HYDRANT

I've said it already, and will say it many more times. God is in charge of all of this. One of the ways this control manifests itself is the way God chooses to appear.

We have to first set aside the question of whether God gets involved in the lives of an individual. This book is founded on the love between individuals and God. Yes, there are lots of people in the world. No, none of us is worthy of God's love. But if you reject the notion that God can be present in people's daily lives, this whole discussion is irrelevant. So, if you read past this point it will be because you are open to the possibility that God will come to you.

In listening to the stories of others, and examining what happened to me, I've concluded that God appears to us according to our needs. Thus, because I had not experienced nurturing, God appeared to me as Holy Spirit, Mother. This does not define God, for the fullness of God is far beyond human comprehension. It's absurd to discuss God's gender, for God has no gender. God is beyond gender, is beyond language, beyond all.

A question you might have had when I mentioned hearing the voice of God, is what language God uses. For me, English, of course. It's the only language I understand. What would be the point of speaking to me in Aramaic, or Latin, or Greek. Don't bother. Communication won't occur.

God speaks to a French mystic in French. So, is God changeable? No, God is greater than any of us can understand. We would really like to confine God to a box of our own construction. "This is what God is, what God wants. Right here, and only here". How lovely. Neat and understandable. And ridiculous. An ant has more comprehension of human existence that humans have of God's.

We harm our own spiritual life, and the lives of others, when we insist that God is only this, or only that. It's understandable that humans want to control God, but it's not only impossible, it's destructive.

God did not appear to me as a talking purple fire hydrant. I would have rejected the experience as wrong, a mistake. That's beyond what I could take in. If God wanted to connect with me, to instruct me, it had to be in a way I could accept.

I believe that's why the God of the Bible is male. Not because God is male, but because in that male-dominated society, a female God would have been rejected as invalid. I on the other hand clung to the skirts of Holy Spirit Mother, who offered me great comfort.

I'm reminded of the story of the blind men and the elephant. Each felt one part of the elephant, and insisted that his was the only correct experience. Mystics will report that God is like this, and God is like that. Their reports tell us more about the mystic's needs than the totality of God.

God will appear differently at different times. During the funeral of a Catholic colleague, I watched as her soul ascended as a beautiful pink rose. The infant Jesus leaned forward in his mothers' arms to receive it. Both he and his mother rejoiced in its presence and beauty. Is Jesus Catholic? An infant? I would answer no and yes to both questions. I was shown that particular vision to comfort me over losing her in this world and to reassure me that we are loved in the next. I also saw how the faithful way she had practiced her religion was celebrated in heaven.

While recently walking in the woods early in the morning, I came upon a young white pine, green and glorious. It stood back-lit in a small glade. I stopped to admire it and suddenly, it was Jesus. I saw again how God is with us, evident in all things. Is Jesus a tree? Yes, and no.

These are gifts, blessings; intended to instruct and comfort. Imagine how poorly it would go over, if I went about proclaiming that Jesus is a tree. God comforted me. That I still need comforting after the great gifts I've been given for so many years tells you something of my condition.

HOLY SPIRIT, MOTHER

Holy Spirit, Mother.
Like an infant calling you -
I am hungry, tiny, helpless.

Crow wings scratch across the sky.
Chickadees flutter near my head,
chirping gently.

I long for you.
In silence,
my soul cries out.

But I am here.
A bubble trapped beneath the surface.
Unable to spring free.

Come for me,
for I know not
how to go to Thee.

Lift me.
Hold me in your arms.

Holy Spirit, Mother
comfort me.

THE RENUNCIATE LIFE

Renounce: to give up or put aside voluntarily

In the context of this discussion, I'm talking about giving up some of the things of this world to support living a more spiritual life. The clearest examples I know are monks and nuns, both Buddhist and Catholic, who are celibate and have no possessions. Living in community, they have renounced much of their identity and status as well. I suspect however that most of them would say they have given up nothing of value, and in fact the tradeoff has greatly benefited them.

Must we give up everything? Why? How can we?

How can I say I am living a Spirit-led life, when I have a wife, children, house and cars?

My answer is both simple, and impossible. The only thing a spiritual life requires is demonstrating our love by <u>paying attention to God</u>. Yet being human we are pre-disposed to pay attention to ourselves. If not our wants, then certainly our hungers.

We will never manage to completely subordinate ourselves. Life has provided us with roles, tasks and responsibilities. I must find my way to God with and through them, not by abandoning what I have been given.

What I need to do is pay attention to God. As much as I can, today. I hope I pay better attention today then I did yesterday, but that's not always true. I succeed, then fail. Pick myself up, turn again and reach for God.

I do this best through spiritual disciplines. Some may prefer the term spiritual practices, but I need the reminder that this is a discipline. It may not be convenient, or what I would prefer at the moment, but it is something I decided on and committed to.

A spiritual discipline is something I agree to try to carry out every day that will help draw my attention to God. It needs to be something that I'm not currently doing, something that requires some thought. It doesn't have to be terribly difficult, but needs to push me out of my normal routines to make some room for God. The particular act is not important, my intention to pay more attention to God is. It can be something as easy and brief as saying to myself, "God's calling," when the phone rings; to a half hour walk I'm not currently doing. In fact, it's better if the act isn't so difficult or repugnant that I just can't force myself to do it every day. All I need to do is shift my attention.

I was introduced to this process years ago. Another key element is that it must be my choice. At first, I took someone else's suggestion of doing daily readings. I just couldn't seem to get into the habit. I wouldn't like the reading I selected, would forget for days, wasn't satisfied with any of the books and so forth.

Fortunately, I gave myself permission to change this discipline that wasn't working. I always made my own lunch for work and chose now to eat peanut butter sandwiches as my new discipline. I didn't hate peanut butter sandwiches, but didn't really like them either. They gave me two chances each day to think about being humble and obedient to God's will – when I made them, and during lunch break.

After a few months, I found that I looked forward to having my peanut butter sandwich. Being quietly brought to God in the midst of a noisy crowded lunchroom became a gift. I continued for many more months, eventually adding another discipline.

The sandwiches had done their task – I was brought closer to God. Day after day, I reflected on humility and obedience. This also happened with all the successful disciplines I've practiced. What at first was awkward eventually became a joy.

The greatest discipline I discovered was the practice of daily prayer. It sounds easy, but hasn't been. I first had to find a consistent time and place when I wouldn't be interrupted. For some reason, I abhor the thought of being intruded upon when I'm praying. Finding a space and time that I controlled was challenging. Three days a week, I traveled between schools during my lunch break. I adopted the practice of driving to a small park, eating quickly in the car and spending about twenty minutes in prayer.

At first it seemed artificial. My comfort grew, and I missed these times on other days. I added the practice of coming to work thirty minutes early, then forty five. Very few people were in the building, and they were doing their own chores.

My connections to God grew and deepened. Prayer went from requiring effort to becoming who I am. I went from an activist stance of "living life as a prayer" to a more passive "being prayer". It is my fervent hope that I pray long and submissively, all the days of my life.

Why should we have to give up anything? I've found that I can't pay attention to more than one thing at a time. Yes, I can chew gum and walk. However, don't talk to me when I'm reading. I'll hear your voice, but unless I stop reading, won't register a word you say. When I worked with children they needed all my attention, knowledge and intellect. I felt that my work with them was a vocation in the religious sense, but I couldn't focus on them and God at the same time.

In the same way, when I focused on my own children, my wife or tasks around the house, I wasn't focused on God. If I was consumed by a love for anything or any one in this world, I wouldn't have any time for God. This is the basis for monks and nuns giving up everything. Freed from the ties of earthly "things", they can be with God all the time.

Some might say, "But I don't want to give up so much." You don't have to. We are free to turn toward God, and away. If all you desire is a quick glance, so be it. God will be there. The question is where you want to be.

SACRIFICES AND BLESSINGS

Strange things happen when we engage in spiritual disciplines. We come to love that which was difficult, for they help us find God. Great blessings may be given to us as well.

JOY

One of my disciplines was gratitude. I gave thanks for whatever I was experiencing, every time I recalled my discipline. I gave thanks for the flower I was passing and the rain. For being forgetful, and the person who was disagreeing with me. For my headache and frustration. Some days I remembered to do this only once or twice, other days perhaps as often as a dozen times.

After several months, I felt something growing in my heart. I was being taught spiritual joy! Deep and constant, based on my connection to a loving God, it began to flow through my soul. Happiness is temporary and dependent on circumstances. Joy lives deeper. Because it's based on a relationship with God, spiritual joy continues, even if it's mixed with tragedy and loss. The spiritual life isn't made up of feeling this or that, but these, simultaneously. Once learned, a constant for me is joy.

You might think that if you meet me, I'll have permanent smile wrinkles. Not so. A stoic Scandinavian, I live as I was taught, with my emotions well wrapped. Nor am I always happy, but even when I contemplate the worst of the human condition, part of my heart is touched by God's love, and rests in joy.

I continued the practice of gratitude for some months, then moved on to a new effort. The joy stayed, and I often give thanks for the blessings that surround me. I particularly try to be grateful when things are going poorly. (I also forget, and get wrapped up in grumbling and feeling sorry for myself.)

FREEDOM

After reading about simplicity, I decided to give away many of my possessions. As a husband/father, most of the stuff in my house isn't truly mine. It also wouldn't be reasonable to give away things that would have to be replaced. So, I ended up getting rid of only a few things like an antique poster and collection of books. I was somewhat attached to them, and had to push myself to let them go. The money I raised from selling them was given away.

Reflecting several weeks later, I was surprised by my feeling of freedom. Although I was still surrounded by stuff, my possessions no longer possessed me. Who I am no longer bears a relationship to what I own. I expend less energy wishing for things. Instead, I have more energy to attend to God.

SERENITY

As captain for a Habitat for Humanity house, I arrived early each work day to prepare for the other volunteers. I soon started arriving fifteen minutes earlier so I could pray. Weeks of submitting to this few minutes of prayer each morning while surrounded with things that needed doing resulted in a sense of serenity. Small at first, it grew to fill me with peace.

Serenity is a spiritual state rarely spoken of or sought after. Yet it is one of the most fulfilling conditions humans can experience. To be at peace with oneself and the world, content to allow history and the future to be as they are. What a marvelous gift!

I deserved none of these blessings. My small, feeble attempts to reach toward God were rewarded a thousand fold. Moreover, these were permanent gifts. I regularly become angry, frustrated, feel sorry for myself, and so on. But, when I come back to who I have become, I find joy, freedom and serenity.

So, naturally, I came to take this process for granted. When I was led to donate a kidney, part of my thinking included wondering what spiritual gift I would be given afterwards. That kind of thinking forced me to re-examine my motivation to make sure my leading was authentic and not based on selfishness. I decided to go ahead with the donation, while recognizing that there was an element of selfishness/wishful thinking involved.

Turns out, that particular act didn't provide me with the kind of blessings I'd been given before. I walked away only with the satisfaction of knowing that when called, I'd answered. While that gives me some confidence that I will be an obedient servant, I also got another lesson in humility and saw again that God is in charge, not me.

The fundamental order of this life is our freedom. We can live as we choose. Ignore God, behave abominably. It's possible. In return for that freedom, we leave heaven to live on this earth, losing most of our wisdom, vision and knowledge of God while living limited lives under the sway of the natural world. We are given an animal self to indulge as we wish.

Knowing God directly breaks these rules. We no longer are free. It is simply not possible to deny God, for God has taken over our awareness, our life. At the same time, we live as flawed humans subject to every disease and disaster. Our consolation is God's love, our joy comes in dying to this world.

HUMILITY

Humility is a necessary condition for travelers on the spiritual path. Not only is it appropriate when approaching Perfection, a cloak of humility keeps us safe. Along with trust, learning humility has been one of the main themes of my spiritual life. I had never thought of myself as an arrogant person, but I hadn't learned abject groveling. That is the position I have come to accept as appropriate for a spiritual supplicant.

When I first beheld Perfect Love, I was overwhelmed. Only much later was I able to process separate aspects of the experience. Along with the ecstasy and gratitude came the beginnings of a sense that I hadn't deserved any of this.

An examination of my 'worthiness' caused me to look at the conditions of my life from a distant perspective. Standing outside myself, I could look down and see my limits and faults. Lifting my eyes, I contrasted this with God's perfection.

The contrast broke my heart.

Which is exactly what needed to happen. First, because it was reality. The difference between

God and human beings is incalculable. My awareness of this fact reinforced the lessons that God's ways don't fit within my former comfortable living. God was in charge, I wasn't. I needed to change, drastically. I needed to listen and accept.

Learning humility served several purposes. It motivated me, for I wish with all my being to love God as thoroughly as I can. To do this, I must become as God wants me to be. I began a long term painful process of rooting around in my depths, lifting up parts of my life. Examining them in the glaring light of God's love, I was often ashamed. And humbled again when I had to ask for God's help in heaving out another hunk of myself.

Eventually, I had done this enough that I began to learn. Strength wasn't what was needed. Acknowledging that I was weak as well as largely helpless and asking for God's help resulted in a lot less pain. Another irony. The world tells us to be strong. God invites us to trust enough to throw ourselves into his arms. There we will find our strength and solace.

Often I was shown my ignorance and pride and consequently prostrated myself, begging for forgiveness. Lying there with my spiritual face in the mud, I could sometimes glimpse another piece of the world as God sees it. When I was brought low, I could see furthest.

I've come to accept that this is one of the rhythms of my spiritual life. I will know periods of tranquility and ease. I will also stumble, and have to go through a cycle of self-examination, requesting forgiveness and seeking guidance. I am forgiven. Amazingly. Always. And I go on, clutching the new understanding humility has delivered.

Humility also keeps me safe, for there are few sign posts on the path. It's possible to get lost and there are siren songs inveigling us to wander off into all sorts of self-deceptions.

For me, the first of these appeared along with my awareness of how much I had been changed by my epiphany experience. If I was different – becoming a better person than I had been – was traveling an unusual path – didn't that mean that I was becoming special? Better? Wiser? More in tune?

More inviting were the powers I glimpsed and thankfully, turned away from. In sharing my experiences with a few people I saw their hunger, and realized I could exploit it through making claims and promises. Although repugnant, the possibilities were there.

How fortunate that I had learned I constantly needed to cling to the hem of God's robe. My response to these temptations was fear, for I had learned to embrace weakness. Immediately, I ran to God and was kept safe. How blessed is humility!

In my daily life, I learned to treasure being slighted. A stock boy working in a grocery isle fails to move to allow me to get past. I am the only customer at the service counter, and the clerk continues shuffling papers. I dress for humility. More than my clothes, my body language has told an 18 year old working for sub-minimum wages that I am not one to fear.

I rejoice, for my outside reflects my inside. I am walking as I should, in humility. I can go about my tasks, praying with those I see in need, open to the miracles and suffering all around me. I am low enough and slow enough that those in need feel free to meet my eyes. We can acknowledge each other's existence and move on.

Learning humility – practicing, failing, practicing some more. Grasping it, clinging to it, finally adopting a posture of humility is necessary. The more parts of me I uncover that are not like God and get rid of, the more room I make for God to come in.

That is my task, my life. A task I will never finish. But after all, the only thing I really need to do. Become a lamp, a transparent shell carrying the Light. Become a bowl, overflowing with Grace. Become a pitcher filled with Mercy. A hollow reed, God's flute. An empty straw, pipeline for forgiveness.

All of them forged through surrender, helplessness, humility.

OBEDIENCE

What a strange notion, for those of us in the first world. Obedience? To whom? Whatever for? Particularly in the United States, freedom is a core value. Except perhaps under extraordinary circumstances, or when in a very few organizations, we don't have to obey anyone.

Or so we'd like to think. There is of course the boss, and several other people in our lives who, if their requests aren't honored, make life difficult. With those insignificant exceptions, we prize our freedom.

There are some requirements on the spiritual path. Without all of them, there's not much of a spiritual journey. Love, humility, listening and obedience. Each supports and teaches the other.

We simply can't relate to God selfishly. Yes we get from God, in abundance. The tiniest spark of God's love breaks open our heart. Turning to that great goodness, our hands automatically open and we become supplicants, asking, "What can I do to ensure that this will continue?" The last thing we want is for

God to turn away or withdraw. If we but knew it, God will never turn or step away.

This love relationship with God also demands that we be honest with ourselves. As Huck Finn said, "You can't pray a lie." There's no way we can hold back, fudge or simply reject God and then blithely run to him/her in prayer. Before we get there, honesty forces us to gather up our newest failure before we confess, shame faced and trembling. The presence of God calls out the best in us. That also means illuminating our worst.

Our lives then are dedicated to an unending quest to grow towards God. The most active portion of that process is listening in prayer, then doing what we understand we should.

This obedience is from God. Terrible things have been done when people listened to another person's message of what God wants. Some Catholic orders taught postulants that obedience to God meant carrying out tasks assigned by a superior, no matter how unpleasant.

I'm not talking about that kind of obedience. The voice of God has come to me through the suggestions of a member of my church. That listening process required that I put aside my thoughts about that person and my relationship with her in order to concentrate on what her soul was saying to mine. It was a worship experience, not a conversation between two people, but two souls, one of which was carrying God's message.

Even then, I pondered it in prayer for days, with little regard for what that person would think. I'd heard the message, and looked for confirmation from God.

Another way of looking at this is that in a spiritual life, God is in control. Typical society thinks that, kind of. On the path, it's real. God talks, we listen and obey. We love, and because we love, we seek to please God. That's it, the essence. Throw in daily prayer as both a form of love and opportunity to receive orders and we have a recipe for living this life in God's heart.

SPIRITUAL POWER

If we do make some kind of spiritual connections, what are we supposed to be doing with them? Should we be seeking some kind of skills or power, to use for some purpose?

During several alternate healing training sessions, I came to know a woman who said she was a shaman. We were both there to learn more about how to help heal people. In listening to her, I reflected on the differences between shamanism and spirituality.

Native Americans had an extensive tradition of shamans who served others with their powers to heal illness and persuade the spirits to bring rain, food and success. Their visions and knowledge were sources of wisdom. While there were standards of behavior that were expected, they were respected primarily for their power. Some were widely believed to be capable of extraordinary things.

I on the other hand, wanted none of this. My path was obedience.

SWEET GRACE

faint breeze
stirs puddle's surface

a thousand facets reflect
God's glory

to be
still
patient
passive

an unworthy bowl
formed of mud

holding
sweet Grace

All I've sought is to be as God wants me to
be. In many visions, I've seen myself as a vessel, an
instrument for God's breath, a simple straw to serve
as a conduit for God's grace. No power, no more
notice than the grass that nourishes the earth.

At the same time, I am open to God's
direction to, "Go there and do this," or "Give people
this message." I am obedient, a servant, a messenger.
I pray it's not I, but the God that lives within me.

This approach is in keeping with traditional Christian spirituality. While incredible tasks may be assigned to an individual – to travel great distances, found great orders – the impetus comes from God, not the person. Then the results are attributed to God as well.

Humility and obedience also serve to keep us safe. It can be heady stuff, to see what others have not seen, be given understandings and offered powers. If we have absorbed the lessons that, "I am one of the least, a servant of the servants," we can stay safe.

For it is possible to get caught up in enthusiasms, mistaking our wishes for God's. In the process, we may mislead not only ourselves, but lead others astray as well. We may even cause great harm.

What I have seen too commonly are forms of spiritual pride. "My spiritual practices or experiences are better than yours."

I admit, I've caught myself being spiritually envious, "I wish that had happened to me. How come to them and not me?" And then things quickly descend to reflections on how unworthy they are and so on.

Ugly, stupid thoughts. All this is God's will, not ours. None of us is worthy. None of us deserve or have earned anything.

There have been many abilities associated with intense spirituality. Christian saints have been said to have gifts of prophecy, biolocation and healing. Some Buddhist monks reportedly can melt snow for many feet in all directions, and transpose themselves through stone walls.

The power of God is beyond comprehension. Anything is possible, and who am I to put limits on God? I have not met anyone who could perform these miracles, but I have glimpsed several lesser gifts. Thank goodness, I was also given the grace to see that these were unimportant distractions.

For several years, I was able to have out of body experiences at will. It was fun, being able to perch on top of a lamp post and it served as another way to view God in nature. I rarely used this gift, and it disappeared.

One of my co-workers showed up at work with a bruise on her face. Part of my job was to relax the tight muscles of special education students. I would prepare for this by pulling a small chair up to the low platform they were laying on . While facing them, I would often still for a minute, seeking to entrain with them. This meant that my back was to the rest of the room, so people couldn't see my face. On this day, I closed my eyes and sent my soul out to my co-worker.

I saw that she had been hit in the face by her husband. He had returned, frustrated, from a hunting trip and had struck her with a rifle's cleaning rod. Later, I gently commiserated with her, letting her know I thought she had been hit by her husband. She denied it, but never showed up at work bruised again. My sense was that she had let her husband know that people at her work were on to him, which caused him to change his behavior.

I assume that I was carrying out God's work. This was the only time I've clearly seen into another's soul.

These brief experiences allowed me to see that many powers are possible. I wanted none of them, and retreated to humility and obedience.

SPIRITUAL INTIMACY

A number of years ago, I was helping lead a retreat. On the last evening, I decided to go and pray in the chapel for one last time. I left my dorm, and when I was about half-way there, met one of the co-leaders walking toward me. She had decided to get a late night snack in the dining room. When she heard what I'd planned, she joined me in going to the chapel, where we sat some distance away from each other.

We had developed a synchrony during the weekend. She was single, I was married with young children. It was dim and quiet, and we were alone. Both Quakers, we were used to worshiping deeply in silence.

And our souls touched. Wordlessly, they entwined. I knew an intimacy, a togetherness, more tender than any I known with another person. It carried echoes of the trust, comfort, knowing and acceptance I'd known with Holy Spirit Mother. After about twenty minutes, we left without discussing what we'd experienced.

She went to her dorm, I to mine. I left early the next morning without seeing her.

For weeks I kept dwelling on what had happened, seeking understanding. It was clear that God had brought us together. It simply could not have been an accident that we both appeared on the sidewalk at that precise time of night. What did it mean? Did God really mean that I should leave my wife and young children, to be with this person I hardly knew? What was it that had transpired between us?

Whatever it was that had happened felt like a blessing, something wonderful. Was I supposed to have this? With her? All the time? But how could I turn my back on my family?

My efforts to understand and thus obey were agonizing. Finally, after about six weeks I prayed aloud, "God this is too painful. I don't understand. I can't go on this way. Please lift this from me."

And God did. I was lifted out of myself so I could see. I had been shown the spiritual intimacy that is possible between two opened souls. In this case, we were to be spiritual friends, period. I saw the wisdom of the monastic tradition that men and woman could not be spiritual advisors for each other. To mix the longing of two souls to join with each other with the possibility of other aspects of a relationship would be too much.

Blessed are those who find a spouse whose souls they can mingle with. I would imagine that this would bring its own hazards as well, and the possibility of great hurt.

I have seen the longing of others whose souls have been opened for spiritual intimacy. I've sometimes sensed their confusion and lack of boundaries about what this hunger is. It's startling to make such quick and deep connections with strangers you've just met. I'm grateful I was taught a context for what these relationships are. I can celebrate them as they occur, secure in the knowledge that I can keep them in bounds.

These are kindred souls, spiritual friends. We can share a special intimacy. In fact, if God has brought us together, we can revel in this rare opportunity to share so deeply. But, these are just friendships. Just because our souls touch so joyfully, no other dimensions to this relationship are implied.

Society talks of finding a "soul mate" when dating. Those whose souls have been opened bring a far different understanding to this term. How ironic that so many of us are not going to experience this soul blending with a mate.

But, if I was to become totally focused on another person in an all-consuming love relationship, where is the space for God? I've heard the statement, "One mystic in a family is enough." I am content to live life on two levels, cherishing those rare times when I encounter a fellow traveler.

TEMPTATION

I wondered for a long time about that line in the Lord's prayer, "Lead us not into temptation." Clearly, God wouldn't lead us into temptation, right? That's the job for the devil (who I don't believe in), or I might lead myself into temptation – something I do every day, if there's any chocolate around.

In the previous example of having been taught spiritual intimacy, it seemed that God had led me into temptation. God had brought me together with this woman, and showed me an intimacy that was soothing, nurturing and enticing. Part of my struggle afterward was not only figuring out what God wanted, but dealing with my hunger.

God tempted me as well by showing me powers. Fortunately, I was also given the grace to see that these were distractions. They were not related to the tasks God had for me, and were thus unimportant, meaningless, even dangerous for me to pursue.

When I now say the Lord's Prayer, I'm sincere in pleading "Lead me not into temptation," for I've seen that God's temptations can be very difficult. They have served as powerful lessons, fierce enough that I will remember what I should not do for a long time.

Besides, I don't need God to tempt me. My physical self provides plenty of temptations, every day.

Some accounts of the lives of saints speak of them despising their hungers and going to great lengths to subdue them. God has treated me far more gently, slowly showing me my errors, allowing me time to learn and change. I know God loves me, just as I am, each moment. That will never change, despite my weaknesses.

I was a drug addict for many years. My drug of choice was nicotine. I tried repeatedly to quit for the last ten years I smoked. After being spiritually awakened, I continued to smoke. Then I became a closet smoker, telling people I'd quit, when in reality I was sneaking several a day. That went on for some time, until I came to see my dishonesty.

I was ashamed. Afraid of what others, particularly other Quakers, would think of me, and ashamed of what I was doing in front of God.

Finally, having seen my behavior for what it was, I was able to quit, when nothing else had worked.

Was I tempted to smoke? Oh yah. Every day for a year. It still happens once in a while, fifteen years later. I shudder when I think back to the days when I was short of breath, and just couldn't control myself. How awful to have some 'thing' in control of your life.

But God didn't make me quit and didn't abandon me when I tried and failed. There I was, having been shown heaven, still addicted. Lying about it. And God loved me. Every day. Always. Addictions don't alienate us from God, but from ourselves. God's arms are the safest place for an addict to be, perhaps the one place they can grow enough to regain themselves.

I've come to see that God made us as we are – souls being carried by animals. There is no shame in desire. The challenges come in behaving correctly.

More than our ordinary human desires is the greatest temptation of all – God. The merest touch of God's love is so beguiling that it can send us off on a chase for more. The desire for God is good. Once we've tasted it, that desire is inevitable. Our hunger may be a big part of what drives us to become holy.

The more we experience God, the more we want. Instead of becoming more aligned with God's will, we can chase ecstasy. It is so wonderful to be immersed in that great love. To experience perfection and taste heaven, for fleeting moments.

Of course we want more. As always, it's our behavior that's the issue. If we forget that God is in charge and try to impose our wants and timetables we get into trouble. "If only I practiced a more rigorous discipline, I can make that happen again." "If only I do something worthy enough, God will reward me."

We can end up as dissatisfied and frustrated about not getting God, as we would be if we wanted material things.

The solution? Humility. Obedience. Gratitude. Trust. "Not my will God, but thine." If we always and everywhere desire nothing but what God wills, we are on the path. God will bring us home, in good time. If it is years before I again know God so sweetly, so be it. All will be well. Best that it be as God wishes.

At a later point in the spiritual life, when our behavior is largely rightly ordered, we are confronted with our desires. I had always thought that the agonizing of the saints over their desires was excessive. After all, God made us as we are, and these are a natural part of being human.

But having known heaven on earth, even if only briefly, I saw the great irony. If I can die to myself, I will fully live. This means suborning not only my will, but my desires. Every particle of us calls out for God, yet we must tell ourselves, "I am nothing. You are everything. I will love you as the grass, the water, the rocks love you."

And so, another whole set of tasks lays before me, work that I will never complete. How wonderful. Self-examination, self-control. Self-love and acceptance. Mixed with glorying in God's creation. Perhaps others can succeed when the way is easy. For me, the steep and rocky path is safest.

SPIRITUAL GROWTH

How does one grow spiritually? What does growth look like – are there three stages, five, or seven, as has been suggested in the literature of the saints? Is the process the same for everyone?

There is no definitive answer, yet people around the globe have been growing spiritually for thousands of years.

I have seen that our souls exist before we are born. When we come to earth, we lose most of our knowledge, wisdom and vision. Our memory of heaven is buried in our soul, barely discernable. Most of us retain a longing for God. I suspect that longing is stronger in some than others. The more we long for God, the easier it is to step away from this world.

That's all we need to grow spiritually – to turn toward God and pay attention. Yet, when there is a three dimensional piece of cake in front of me, as well as all the other elements of this life, how can I attach my attention to something I can't see, or touch, or hear? And what of the legitimate demands on my attention – responsibilities, tasks, relationships?

The hard fact is that the less attached you are to this world, the more attached you can be to God. Hermits don't go into the desert to run away from the world, but to run toward God. There's a reason monks and nuns are single, own nothing, and live in cloisters.

But what about the rest of us who can't or aren't ready to drop connections to this world? Is there anything we can do?

We can all begin where we are. Just where we are, today. And if tomorrow we mess up and feel even further from God, we can begin there. Wherever we are, whenever we can.

I feel most comfortable dividing spiritual growth into three steps – seeking, contemplation and union. They can not be cleanly delineated. People move back and forth between them, often within a single day. Where someone starts and ends up differs as well. For now, let's try to define each.

SEEKING

When I think of people on spiritual journeys, the groups that come first to mind are Buddhists. From the outside, it looks to me as if they frequently make time to push aside what "is" in order to seek the other reality. As they practice for years, they grow in depth and wisdom. Some Jews, Christians and Muslims pursue life-consuming spiritual paths as monks, nuns, teachers, scholars and religious leaders. Buddhists seem to invite all their adherents onto the path, encouraging them to go as far as they are able.

What can Westerners who aren't full time religious personnel do? We can make some room for God in our lives – even if it's just a little. Daily prayer for fifteen or even five minutes that includes some time for listening. An open heart, turned toward God, will be filled. When it's overflowing, growth will follow.

The touch of God's grace is so healing, merciful and loving that we will become more faithful in our prayer life and our priorities will begin to shift. Slowly, we will open to God as a flower opens in the spring. Will we encounter storms and contract? Yes, but as long as we continue to come back to prayer, we will grow.

We will begin to seek to please God, striving to hold up a particle of ourselves worthy of sharing with the mercy poured upon us. Our efforts toward self-control, moderation, right living, justice and compassion will be reflected. We will see, and begin to understand, and be inspired.

More than this, we will be loved. Loved as we never dreamed was possible.

We will face challenges, seeing issues within ourselves that stand between us and more fully embracing God. These will become more painful as we struggle to reach around and over them to get to the great love we increasingly can't live without. Each of us will have burdens – brokenness, lusts, addictions – that we will probably struggle to overcome for the rest of our lives.

We will also be presented with lessons tailored to our personalities, histories and burdens that we will never fully learn in this life. For me, these have included humility, trust and obedience.

God will have work for us. Some tasks will be joyful. Others will be painful, frightening, repugnant. After completing many of these, we will become used to the idea of being yoked to God's will – a servant of the servants of the Lord.

Often we will see God's fingerprints in our lives only when we look back and notice the slow progression of what must happen. We are shrinking within our own lives, and God is growing.

CONTEMPLATION

As our awareness of God's presence in our lives grows, we begin to see God in the world surrounding us. Our lives have become unusual as we shift more and more to God as the center of our existence.

No more is God confined to the few minutes we persuaded ourselves to spend in prayer every day. Now, we see God in a child's smile and the perfect curve of a flower petal. A pothole in the road reminds us of that time we fell on our face and God laughingly picked us up. The road sign swaying in the wind makes us think of God's spirit flowing through us, and we rejoice.

Life has become a prayer. Slowly, gradually, we've lost control, beguiled by Love. None of this is done for rewards or the fear of God's wrath. We are dancing, the joyful wriggling of an infant held in its mother's arms and basking in her smile.

Which is not to say that any of this is easy or understandable. Life continues to beset us, and we remain in its clutches. We have no idea what will happen next, and frequently disappoint ourselves. At times joyful, we are also deeply grieved by our unworthiness and limitations. We step forward, then step back and might make progress only after throwing up our hands and admitting we are helpless.

Still, if we are fortunate and it is God's will, we progress month by month, year by year; growing in love, joy, peace and compassion. We remain limited and damaged but become less absorbed by self.

As we progress, trust grows. We loosen our grasp on God's hem, and slowly surrender to God's will and God's time. Paradoxically, God will come to us more fully as we let go and desire to simply obey and be.

I believe everyone can know the joys of a contemplative life while continuing to live in the world. Worthy work, community service and membership in families can all be done well by

131

someone whose heart and soul are focused on God. Greed, domination, status seeking and violence would have to shrink. While normal societal values would be largely irrelevant, we can live full lives in the midst of this world.

This stage of life can be marvelous and never ending. There is always more to learn and growing to do. As we subdue our will our joy grows. This is the secret, the great secret of a spiritual life. The greatest secret of our human existence. To love God and to seek only God's will is to find joy. A deep joy that flows on despite the pain and loss of this world.

UNION

This stage is less common. It can occur after prolonged, strenuous effort to empty oneself of self while sinking deeper into the Other. It can also occur in an instant, if God comes to us.

In contemplation, when we see God in the things around us, our soul can flow out to that reality, and we know that we are one with all that is. This is a form of union, for contemplation blends with union. These experiences leave us hungry for more, and we begin to long for God.

I have seen this process frustrate many people. They want an experience of God that they expect – to hear God's voice or touch, or have a vision. They may look at a leaf and see through to the other side, then denigrate their own experience because God didn't speak to them.

We need to surrender to God's will. What will happen, will happen. Wanting more, wanting now puts us in our own way. "I want, I expect," must give way to, "Thy will be done." Looking back, I rejoice that I so often practiced gratitude, for it helped me joyfully align myself with what had happened, and opened me to what could be.

In our typical lives, we are rewarded for taking charge, being active, making things happen. Here, we need to be passive, helpless, patient; our soul a fetus lying in God's heart.

Like a fern in the spring, we need to open ourselves, then stand, widespread and open. If it's cloudy, we rejoice. We bless the rain, and we are there; just there, should God decide to shine fully upon us.

How easy, and impossible, to die to self. Surrendering expectations, needs, even hopes. Letting go and letting go, as much as we can. Tiny steps seemingly leading to what? There are no guarantees except that a great love waits for us; more and more, if we can just let go.

God can also break through in an instant to someone who has spent little time on the spiritual path. There was one constant in the lives of people I've talked to and read about who have had an epiphany experience. It was true for me as well. God came at a moment when they were utterly broken. Not merely scared or faced with the death of a loved one, but shattered. Only after they had no hope, no basis for going on. Out of their despair, God came.

Why? Why couldn't God have come sooner, under less excruciating circumstances? Why not grant more people this great gift?

Because they weren't ready to go through the steps of listening, losing their freedom, and dying to this world. God came only when they had reached the point of acknowledging that they could not going on living as they were. And so God came and ended life as they had known it. In a wonderful, marvelous, blessed way. But ended it forever.

Meeting God means losing your typical human existence. There can be no doubts about God's existence. Encountering overwhelming Love means we can't turn away. The center of our universe has shifted from us to the Other. Everything and everyone else is subordinate. Disappointing our new love becomes our greatest fear and we no longer belong to ourselves.

The physical stimulus that initiated the epiphany may have been as simple as seeing a drop of rain on a leaf. If someone leading a typical life had such an experience, they would almost certainly reject it. How could they abandon all that they know because they caught a fleeting glimpse of something?

Those who are ready to listen, cling. There are no regrets, only joy at having been delivered. They view the resulting changes in their lives with wonder, certain in the knowledge that they are now different, detached. I experienced this as relearning everything I thought was true, while gazing at the earth from somewhere far off in the cosmos.

An epiphany is a lesson – life changing and transformative. The individual's work has only begun. We want every particle of our life, our selves, to resonate in perfect harmony with God. Then we look down at ourselves and are filled with despair at how flawed, damaged and limited we are. God soothes, teaches, challenges us over and over.

There may be those who reach some stage of perfection in this life. I'm not one of them. I suspect I'll be berating myself on my death bed for things done poorly and left undone and a long list of imperfections.

I've met one person whose life is an exception to the stages of spiritual growth we've been discussing. That's to be expected, since we are only dim observers of God's work. Much as we'd like there to be rules, steps and clear expectations, God is in charge.

A mom brought her young son to our Quaker Meeting, saying she wanted to find a spiritual home for him. I was often the Sunday school teacher, and got to know him. He talked about seeing angels and spirits throughout the day, but particularly in his bedroom at night. This had been happening since he was about four years old. He was eight when I met him. His mother confirmed that he often talked of seeing beings. They reassured him and he was comfortable with them.

I am a pediatric Occupational Therapist with training and experience in childhood disabilities, including mental illness. In listening closely, it appeared to me that this was a perfectly normal child who just happened to be in frequent contact with the spiritual world. I was able to reassure his mother – the boy didn't need a reassuring. We welcomed the two of them and they met with us for six months, until they moved out of town.

Talk about unfair. This little boy routinely had experiences that others strive for – long for – all their lives. Things they may or may not receive after years of struggle were freely given to him.

But that's God's will, not ours. 'Why' is not for us. In thinking back, I'm concerned for him. Struggle, failure and self-discipline help teach us humility and obedience. The gift without the container is potentially dangerous. I pray that he doesn't misunderstand the gifts he's been given, or worse yet, misuses them.

SPOUSES

What if you came home and told your spouse/partner, "I had the most wonderful experience at church today. I fell madly in love with someone. My mind, my heart, my very soul is filled with their presence. I'm sure that from now on, I will think of them constantly and would follow them to the ends of the earth."

Would your partner/spouse be thrilled? If you told them it was God you were talking about, would that make it acceptable? Anywhere near as wonderful as you were feeling about this new reality?

That hasn't been my observation. The sudden intrusion of God between a couple has led to confusion, fear and distance. Where there were only two people, now there are three. Assumptions, priorities and power within the relationship need to be reassessed.

But how can they be? If it was an epiphany experience, the person is dazed and overwhelmed. Unable to comprehend or communicate what has happened, they can offer no clarity or reassurance. If it has been a gradual process, the spiritual (weird) partner may be able to communicate about their growth experiences. In neither case can they offer certainties about what God has in store for them in the future.

None of this is reassuring to the non-mystical (normal) spouse, who wants life to go on as it should – meaning like they expected it to be, and like everybody else around them. They didn't sign up for this strange stuff, and don't want to share their spouse's affections or – truth be told, as God's presence grows – see their spouse/partner loving someone else more.

If they were involved with another person, we would call this emotional infidelity. Because God is involved, it also could be said to be spiritual infidelity.

I've seen spiritual growth contribute to distance in marriages and divorce. Many of the deeply spiritual people I've met have been single, and their spirituality appears to be an obstacle to forming encompassing relationships with another person.

What's the deal? Is being single something God requires? Desires? Obviously, it's not something required, for epiphany experiences and gradual spiritual growth happen all the time to people who are in relationships. What God requires of us is paying attention.

I have met happily married couples who are both also deeply spiritual. They are greatly blessed.

It seems to me that it would be difficult for an individual in a wonderful relationship where neither person is spiritual to allow enough room in their life for God. If someone's attention, heart and being are filled with the presence of their spouse, it would be very difficult to turn away from them and focus on God. If both people moved toward God and spiritual growth was an organic part of their relationship, it could be a smooth transition.

More common are instances where one partner was not wholly entranced with their partner, and thus had the energy and hunger to bring to a relationship with God. Being single or in relationship isn't the issue. We must be available – ready to listen to a voice that at first may seem incredibly faint and abstract. Willing to cling tightly to this new found world, and begin the process of loosening our ties with our physical surroundings.

Beginning the spiritual path requires letting go. If our partner comes with us, we can travel together. If they aren't willing to step on the path, we have to be willing to go on without them. We don't need to get divorced, but we will create differences and space between us and our loved one.

We naturally want to share the most important parts of our lives with our partners. When life with the One becomes the ground of our being, we many hunger for a partner who understands and treasures the same reality. Dumping a non-spiritual partner to go in search of a kindred soul is foolish, selfish and self-defeating.

Acting on 'I want' without regard to the feelings or well being of family members is wrong. Acting wrongly puts us squarely in our own way in our relationship to God. Just as right living keeps us tucked warmly in God's heart, wrong living alienates us. As always, we need to ask for guidance, and obey.

I have known people who feel terribly isolated and lonely because neither their partner nor their community is open to spiritual communion. Some have known a great deal of suffering from this isolation. Yet, that hunger can itself help propel us into God's arms.

Spiritual singles can find it difficult to find an appropriate partner. A hunger for intimacy encompassing not only the intellectual, emotional and physical but spiritual as well is hard to fulfill. Many spiritual people settle for staying single. If their soul can't mingle with a potential partner's they won't go ahead.

Spirituality at first glance seems marvelous. Just think, getting to hang out with God, basking in this great love day after day. In practice, it isn't easy at all. Dying to ourselves, dying to this world takes great effort. At times, it involves great pain and loss. Rarely is it just as we wish it was. The essence of our efforts is to submit to God's will. In the context of our closest familial relationships, that can be most challenging.

Patience, hope, surrender, prayer can carry us.

CONVERT

All right, I'm through with whining –
         for today.

For years I lived crouched
in a bubble frosted
with my intestines – torn out and smeared
to shut out what I couldn't stand.

I found a way out.
Others, then You helping.
and stood squinting, amazed
at sun and flower petals and butterflies.

You warned me.

Showed me a horrendous pain
and asked if I would pick it up.

Reluctantly, I said yes,
thinking it would be physical, public –
noble perhaps.

Hah!

So now I've cried for two weeks
and screamed inside my head so loud
that I will ride that sound for years.

And in silence I've converted
a life times' loss

without needing to know why.

SEX

Right living sexually can be summed up by applying an understanding we already have. If you're living in obedience to God's will, and you are comfortable inviting God in to witness a sexual encounter, you're OK.

At first, it's a startling idea – God watching you have sex. If God is everywhere and omniscient, the conclusion is clear – God watches everything we do. There's no hiding, no secrets. Even unspoken motivations are laid bare in the glare of truth.

Fortunately, God is also merciful. So many times when I've criticized myself for being all too human, along with God's forgiveness has come an understanding that I am, after all, human. God made me the way I am, and understands that I have human hungers and needs. Until I fly from the limitations and demands of this physical shell, there will be many times when my humanity takes precedence over holiness.

Sex is one of God's greatest gifts. Like any great gift, it has great potential. It can appropriately address so many needs – comforting, affirming, sharing, communicating, pleasure. Exploitation,

144

coercion, deception and manipulation are inappropriate. Casual sex risks not just health, but numbing the emotions and soul. A great gift can become merely a form of exercise.

Sex can become terribly distorted when freighted with burdens. Self-worth, self-identity, healing or finding life's meaning will probably not be achieved with sex as a primary mechanism. It's likely that such attempts will not only fail, but will create problems larger than the original need.

Is it OK for one partner to use another? Yes, if both understand that there is a giving and receiving, and both are comfortable with what is suggested. Unhealthy relationships, where one person is always giving and the other taking will result in unhealthy sex. The base problem is the quality of the relationship, and each person's lack of emotional health.

Neither can God/spirituality be used as an excuse to stop having sex with a partner. I've heard that Gandhi adopted the practice of celibacy, long after he was married. My first thought was whether his wife had an opportunity to participate in that decision. Maybe she was thrilled, or felt betrayed.

The stories always concentrated on him, so I have no idea.

Committed partnerships are just that – partnerships. Neither person has the right to unilaterally make significant changes. Or if they do, they can't expect their partner to accept the change. The relationship itself may be put in jeopardy. Difficulties with the sexual aspects of a relationship have to be worked out without hiding behind God.

Is masturbation or using pornography within a committed relationship wrong? I don't know. When is it OK to have sex in a new relationship? Those are questions for God. You can't turn your back and avoid the effects your behavior will have on your relationship with God, so you might as well ask. How wonderful, if you and your partner can pray together for an answer.

God's answer may well be different for different people, or at different times.

Ask, and obey.

EVIL

I know nothing of the Devil. In my spiritual travels, I have encountered only good. There is no need for a devil. The vagaries of the natural world and human being's potential for evil are adequate to account for bad things happening.

I've been fortunate to have the opportunity to travel repeatedly in the Boundary Waters Canoe Area Wilderness in Northern Minnesota. Although most of it was logged over a century ago, since then it's been left largely alone. Everywhere you look, you can see what nature intends.

The pines reseeded themselves abundantly. Some of the seeds landed in cracks in boulders that held a little dirt. I never tire of looking at how those tree's roots meander and writhe over bare rock in an effort to find sustenance. Often, trees die when still quite young. It became clear to me that mother nature is profligate with her progeny. Continuation of the species happens through widespread trial – and errors. Nature is indifferent to the life of individuals.

Thus it is with the volcano, hurricane, tidal wave. They happen, and those who live close by, die.

This isn't evil, it's the natural world. Drought and floods kill, disease strikes anywhere. It's the way the world is made – harsh and capricious.

The movement of tectonic plates will cause earthquakes, which if they occur under or near the ocean will cause tidal waves. That's the way the earth is made, and those processes have been going on for billions of years. To blame the process doesn't make much sense. It's understandable that we think like this, for we put ourselves at the center of the universe, feeling we are the only reason anything should occur. Our limited vision, bound in egocentricity, causes us to see the natural world as it effects us. We label events accordingly.

We often go one step further, and blame God for what happened. But who made the choice to live above an earthquake fault; near an ocean subject to hurricanes or tidal waves; in a river valley subject to floods? Some natural events are inevitable. Any particular spot in the American Midwest could be hit by a tornado. Perhaps not this century, the last or the next, but it will happen. Why not this year? Why not your house?

If we don't blame God, we may blame evil or the devil. But isn't that the same thing as blaming God?

The God I know is all powerful. Nothing can happen without God's knowledge or against God's will. To believe that there is some force causing things to happen that God can't control is to believe in a small God. One who is not all powerful. One who could not have created the universe, and couldn't possibly reach into the lives of an individual.

I reject those notions. God is all powerful, all knowing, present everywhere and always. Nothing happens that God does not know about and allows to happen.

To believe in the Devil is to believe in a schizophrenic God who allows a subordinate to do bad things. I don't believe in hell either (we'll talk more about that later). But we're talking about the present world here, not the afterlife. God is either in charge, or he/she isn't. You have to make up your mind.

Having never known anything but a God of love: merciful, boundless, intimate, patient and forgiving; I reject the notion of a Devil, or any other malignant force.

Our forbearers where familiar with death. Even young children witnessed siblings die. People lived at the mercy of their surroundings. Hot or cold; wet or dry; eat or starve were beyond their control. For most westerners, death has been pushed to the corner, where it can be ignored. Modern lifestyles allow the illusion of control. Except for an occasional camping trip or extraordinary circumstance, most of us feel we are the masters of our environment.

When our illusion is shattered by an accident or illness, we have no context. "This wasn't supposed to happen," is our common response. But of course, the tree branch falls according to the biology of rotted wood, wind pressure and gravity. It must, for things in this world must obey the natural law. It will fall with a great deal of force, and smash what or whomever is under it at that moment.

Life is short, and isn't fair either. No one leaves this world alive. We can take the stance that things shouldn't be this way and live in fear and resentment. Or, we can see each day as a gift, an opportunity to grow in love and obedience. Either way, if we are standing under the tree branch, we'll get squished.

Most disasters fall most heavily on the poor. The fewer resources they have, the more they suffer. The drought, flood, hurricane, epidemic follow nature's course. Their effect however is disproportional.

Here we have the interaction of a harsh world with human failings. No, I'm not blaming the poor. Most of us, if we were born and raised on the banks of a river, would stay. Especially if we had few resources. My criticism is for those who have resources and use them for their own benefit. If the rich had put less into building their hill top homes and more into flood prevention, education and appropriate housing for the poor, the effects of a flood could have been minimized.

But few societies or governments place the safety of the very poor as a high priority. Who bears the responsibility for their resulting deaths during a natural disaster? Not God, if humans could have averted them.

By far the biggest evils have been from human, not natural origins. War and genocide caused tens of millions of deaths in the last century. There is no need for a Devil, some "other" that brings evil to this world. I carry within myself the capacity to cause great harm. All that is necessary is to turn loose my "animal" self.

I don't believe people are born evil. The notion of original sin, a condition we have to be rescued from, leaves me unconvinced. From before we are born, our being is joined with God. We carry that divine spark with us through this life, imbuing our lives with holiness, whether we know it or not. This is true for all people, everywhere.

For the short time we spend on this planet, our holiness is wrapped in an animal. We retain the instincts that perpetuated our animal ancestors. Dominance, procreation, territoriality, aggression, predation are part of our biological makeup. Can we control them? We must, or render ourselves unfit to live in society.

I feed the birds each winter. Watching them flutter above the blank background of a snowy landscape reminds me that life goes on. They aren't there for entertainment however, but survival. Larger birds chase off the smaller and are chased off in turn by larger species. There is no compassion for a weaker, hungrier companion. Strength wins.

In the spring, the bird calls I so enjoy are attempts both to be more attractive to a mate and to establish a territory where other males may not go. If boundaries are violated a fight ensues, with the stronger the victor.

All these urges exist in me. I want status, to procreate, defend my territory, acquire and take from others. I recognize vulnerability and am attracted to it, as a predator to the laggard. We may label them differently in humans – vanity, lust, greed, aggression – but they have their origins at the bird feeder.

All that is needed for great evil to occur is for one or more people to turn these behaviors loose, disregarding the well-being of those they victimize.

Perhaps one of the greatest human skills is empathy – an ability to recognize the feelings of others, including when they are different from our own. A companion virtue is compassion – being with, and caring about others. If all we need for evil to occur is to loose our animal selves, then empathy and compassion are the antidote. There are laws and social expectations that may constrain our harmful behaviors, but deeper than these is the positive of caring for each other.

Mankind's animal natures have led to immediate evils. Our limitations lead us to more insidious long term hideous outcomes. Millions of people – many of them children – go hungry. Tens of thousands die from the effects of malnutrition every day. Poverty, ignorance and disease are the norm in many parts of the world.

And we do next to nothing.

Perhaps a quarter of all females in the United States are sexually assaulted at some time in their life. Thousands of children are abused and neglected. The homeless inhabit all our cities; many of them veterans or mentally ill.

And we do next to nothing.

For these people are somehow different, perhaps deserving of their fate. Our lives are not like that, which surely makes us more competent. Perhaps it's even a sign of our worthiness that we have so much, and their unworthiness that they have so little. It was meant to be. The more I can think of them as different, responsible for their circumstances, the more I can deny that the same thing may happen to me or my family.

And what would you have me do about it anyway? Charity begins at home (would you like to see the new carpet)? It's the job of parents to give their children a good future, which surely includes the best neighborhood and every opportunity.

This blend of animal desires (status, greed) mixed with positive goals (the well being of our children) produces a set of values that serve us well. By maintaining some distance (those starving children live somewhere else, who knows where) and ignoring the occasional inconvenient homeless person, we live our lives cocooned in a materialistic bubble.

We don't need to be actively contributing to the misery of others. Our indifference is all that is needed for it to continue.

What incredible arrogance we display! The death of a toddler in Africa, whose parents lacked shelter, access to medical care, water or food means a spark of God that was on this earth was rejected. We forget – we can't get our heads wrapped around

155

– the notion that in God's eyes, all are equal. That child's life was as important to God as ours.

The One grieves the untimely death of that child and the circumstances of his family. God also grieves for us who did so little.

What? We had nothing to do with that child's death. In fact, we gave some money to an international charity. Just last month. About .0001% of our income. Am I to be my brother's keeper? Mess up my life by making huge sacrifices, just to help people I've never met? I didn't create their difficult circumstances. I can't be held responsible for fixing them.

I have seen in several visions that we are all one. There is no us and them, no you and me. There is only us. All of us, resting together in God's heart. We were there in God's heart before we were born, continue that connection (although we aren't aware of it) when we are on this earth, and will return. I am not only my brother's keeper, I am my brother and sister.

Why are we on this earth? Is it to become 'self-actualized'? To grab as much pleasure, status, power and possessions as we can?

Some are born with little, some with much. Some live in dangerous places, others in safety. It is the task for those of us with resources, to assist those without. The lives of Mother Theresa and Gandhi were not aberrations. That's how all of us are supposed to live – in service to others. I'm talking about an uncomfortable level of sacrifice. Choosing to spend all or part of our vocational lives in service. Giving away so much money that we can't afford a second car thus inconveniencing ourselves and our family. Discussing whether it would be better to pay for a child's lessons, or give that amount of additional money away. Spending leisure time volunteering.

In a material sense, living small. In a broader sense, living as God would have us live. Unusual? Yes. Difficult? Yes. Uncomfortable as well, because we are turning our backs on 'things' that are right in front of us, in order to assist those we don't know, for reasons we can't see.

As the only mystic in the family, I can't live this radically. The rest of my family wouldn't see things the way I do. Given a choice between leaving or staying and serving how I can, I'm staying. My sense is that I'm doing with my life what God wants.

But I don't rail against the injustice of nature or blame God. I know that much of the world's suffering could be alleviated if many people understood and lived accordingly.

What a magnificent world we live in. The life cycle of a carrot is a miracle. How can such a tiny seed send its roots and stem in the right directions? And turn into food, so many times larger? A hillside painted with fall leaves can leave us breathless with its beauty. Babies' peaceful sleep shows hints of an angelic presence.

What an awful world God made. The natural world drowns, burns, crushes the innocent. People add their measures of evil and indifference and horror ensues.

I frequently say a prayer of thanks for the opportunity to live in such a magnificent, awful world. I see this as the celestial bargain. I'm given my freedom to live as I wish on this earth. In return, my life is subject to the natural law. I can choose to grab all I can, or live as God wishes – in service to others.

I saw a slide show years ago by a couple who had traveled to China. One slide showed a man hoeing a rice field. It was about one acre – the size of a modest American yard. His whole life was and would be bound by that one acre plot of mud. It was the task that life had given him.

I often think of that when I ask God for guidance. For that's what I seek – my small task. Mine is not to do big things, but to do what I can for others, and cause no harm in the process. Seemingly simple, sometimes joyful, but impossible to do perfectly.

I have room to grow.

PRAYER

Prayer is not a discrete entity, but a complex banquet which in the end becomes self-sustaining and if we're fortunate, consumes us.

Our intent often determines the form of the prayer. It's easy to get nonplussed by an unfamiliar form of prayer, something we can't relate to and want nothing to do with. But it's the intent that is more important and universal.

I have no interest in drumming, chanting or singing as forms of prayer. I do enjoy meditating while cross stitching and wood carving. Do you condemn me for this? How about if instead, I chanted, "Ohm"? Imposing our form of prayer on another is as inappropriate as condemning theirs. You pray in a manner that works for you. I'll do the same. Just don't begin drumming in the midst of my silent time. We'll need separate spaces for that – well away from each other.

Why are we praying? Do we want to get something from God, hear from God, or be with God? These are quite different ends.

INTERCESSORY PRAYER

Many many people engage in intercessory prayers, particularly in times of crises. "Lord, please ...." The desires can be very laudable - someone's health - or minor such as hitting a homerun. It's been said that there are no atheists on the battlefield, and that's understandable. When faced with great danger, God is the only one who can help.

It saddens me to watch Harry Potter movies or read the books. Their emphasis on magical beings isn't anti religious, but it is utterly nonreligious. To see a child face death – alone – and not be able to call on God is tragic. I think the books are an accurate reflection of a secular lifestyle that does not deny God's existence, but has concluded that the Divine is irrelevant, unimportant. Not worth thinking about and a waste of time.

How awful, to face this natural world with no one to help. We may not face magical creatures, but difficulties, accidents, disasters and illness will be known to us all.

There's nothing wrong with asking God for help. We will all need it throughout our lifetimes. There continue to be times when I "tell God what to do", and other times when I've moved beyond this.

There is an element of the absurd in asking God for what we want. We're requesting that no matter what nature/the natural law has in store for us, or God has in mind, we want what we want. We're demonstrating selfishness and arrogance (again). But, we're human. We do want what we want. Our vision is limited. I continue to pray for what I believe is best for people close to me, asking for God's mercy. I'm confident that God receives those prayers in the spirit they're intended.

And there's a question. How selfish is whatever I'm asking for? Requesting success in business, sports, relationships may be quite self-centered. They are also an opportunity to step back and examine how badly and why we want those things. Intercessory prayers become not only a way for us to ask for things, but a window to examine ourselves.

How arrogant am I? Do I trust God? Am I willing to submit to God's will? A little? A lot? Then why am I asking for specific outcomes? Can I move toward saying, "Thy will be done?"

I can move further in submitting to God's will when it's a personal issue than when I view the well being of friends and family. Then I want healthy pleasant outcomes in this world, now. That's a reflection of the limitations of my faith I suppose. God's way is the best for everyone, always, in the long run. I'm greedy, and want the best for my children.

So, while I continue to sometimes ask God for specific outcomes, more and more often I ask simply for mercy. We're in trouble if all we get from God is justice. What we need is forgiveness and another chance we don't deserve. Quakers have a phrase for this process – holding others in the Light. I like that image, of holding someone in prayer, watching while God's love is poured upon them.

For a long time, when I saw someone in unfortunate circumstances, I prayed for them. Whether homeless, or simply appearing unhappy in the grocery store, I prayed for their well being. A friend introduced me to praying each time I heard the siren of an emergency vehicle for the safety of those in the vehicle, and those being served.

I came to see that I was holding myself as better than these others – better off, safer, separate, different. Magnificent me, deigning to help these unfortunates. Not true. I am them. God loves them in a measure equal to God's love for me. It is only arrogance and blindness that makes me think I am better than the ragged, filthy homeless person huddled in that doorway. Moreover, by holding myself above them, I kept myself out of the stream of love being poured out for them.

I began to pray that God would be with both of us, would have mercy on both of us. I see myself with them, equally in need of God's help and bound with them by God's love. How blessed, to spend time seeing both of us bathed in grace that descends bountifully. It is the 'being with' I bring to the process that enhances the whole.

Does it do them any good? I believe it does. God was with them, is with them always. My bringing the particle I carry of God's presence to be with theirs warms us both. I can not shelter the homeless, feed the hungry or cure the ill. I lack the means and those tasks weren't given to me. What I can do is be with them, deeply.

I've had a number of people tell me that they know that I'm praying for them, and that my prayers help. These have been spiritually aware people, some of whom are half a continent away. Neither distance nor circumstance separates us, any of us. We can touch each other's souls. When we first submerge ourselves in God, we can then companion and comfort others.

Are our prayers a substitute for action? Is it OK for me to merely pray for the hungry while failing to do anything to assist them?

One task can not substitute for another. If God calls me to work in a food bank I'd better get there and do what I can. If instead, God tells me not to work in the food bank but to pray for those in my community who are hungry, I should do that. Of course, while I'm working in the food bank, I can also pray to be with those who I'm serving. What I can't do is deceive myself that I can avoid acting as I should just because I'm praying.

HEARING FROM GOD – PRAYERS OF DISCERNMENT

If one part of prayer is to tell God what we want, another part is to listen to what God wants of us. Should we do this or that? Go, or stay? Sometimes we can know clearly, in fact we can be commanded. At other times, we have only the faintest inkling, or none at all. We can make mistakes too, misunderstanding and subsequently failing. The important thing is to ask, to wait, to care about what God wants. Everything else will work out in the end.

The question, "Does the end justify the means?" is incorrect, for the means is the end. Our part is to proceed compassionately wherever we are led. The outcomes are in God's hands. To ask, turn in the indicated direction and go forth with humility and love. We are required to use all the gifts God has given us – our intelligence, knowledge and skills. Success isn't the only criterion. If we end up making an ass of ourselves and utterly fail it's OK.

I remember how I learned God has a sense of humor. Many years ago, I had a vision of a golden pencil. This vision brought me the understanding that I was to write. I had been writing poems, and promptly sent several of them to a Quaker journal for publication. They were quickly rejected.

I crawled into worship the next Sunday, ashamed to show my face before God because I had failed. I was lifted up and stood shoulder to shoulder with Jesus, while we reviewed my efforts from on high. We both laughed to see how feeble and limited I am in my human guise, and how silly it is to be preoccupied with outcomes. Moreover, how thoroughly we deceive ourselves that we can control our surroundings. Filled with God's love, I learned not to fear failure. I fail only if I am not obedient either in taking up a task – or failing to refuse that which is not mine. All too often, I also fail when I don't carry out tasks lovingly.

While outcomes are not ours, tasks are. Nor can we see into the future. So many times, I have seen in retrospect how an outcome has helped lead me to where I am, where I am supposed to be.

In the long run, we simply don't know the results of what happens today. As contemporary first world citizens, we can deceive ourselves that we are in control of our lives. True, young children no longer routinely die and wolves rarely invade our backyards to slaughter our livestock. We'd like to be in charge, to be able to hold death and misfortune at bay because we have all the accoutrements of modern society at our finger tips.

God is still in charge. Always. We are given a great deal of freedom and opportunity. Far better for us if we offer all that back to God. "Thy will be done," repeated again and again each day will keep us on the path and align our efforts with God's.

How are we to know what God wants? We have to ask and wait for an answer. It may well be that "wait" is the answer we get. Human beings want solutions, want action now. God's time is often slower and more deliberate. Patience is the first requirement.

We may be given clear answers. Rarely, I have heard the voice of God. More often I get a sense of rightness, a certainty that I should proceed. If I don't get this sense of rightness I've learned to wait, if that's possible. Some situations are time limited, and I'm faced with the dilemma of acting without permission, or letting the opportunity go by.

It wasn't uncommon for me in my early spiritual days to engage in prayers of whining. One of those prayers included a complaint that I hadn't been told whether or not to proceed with some question I've now forgotten. This was one of the times God spoke directly to me. In answer to my, "Why won't you tell me what I should do," God answered, "That's why I gave you a brain." I took that to heart, and in the absence of any guidance, have come to rely on my best judgment in determining what would be the most loving thing to do.

During periods when I'm waiting for an answer from God, sometimes for many days, I pay attention to my surroundings. I might carry a question in the forefront of my mind while I take a prayer walk in a park. The scream of a raptor or rustle of last year's weeds may pull me out of myself to a place that provides insight and a broader perspective. So often, I realize that my view of circumstances is terribly limited.

I can also get answers through other people. Once during a retreat, I'd spent time during a group prayer imploring God for guidance. Afterward, I shared the issue with another participant. He offered several observations. This was the last activity of the night, so I decided to go for a walk. Praying under the stars, I asked why I wasn't getting an answer. God replied, "Who do you think you were just talking to?"

I learned in that instant that God can and does talk directly to us through other people. During times when I'm searching for guidance, when someone speaks to me about the issue at hand, I listen hard. Are their words coming from a deep place? Do I feel a trusting, comfortable connection with this person? If so, I take what they have to say very seriously, pondering it until I develop a sense of whether or not what they shared was a message from God.

Where does all this leave us? In the soup. That wonderful complex unpredictable spiritual life where God's in charge, and we don't know what's going on. We first of all need to care about what God wants. Then all we need do is ask, wait, and proceed as best we can, secure in the knowledge that we may fail, stumble or succeed. If we go forth in humility and love, all will be well.

FORMS OF PRAYER

I have to admit that I know very little about how to pray. During the first years after my epiphany experience, I often experienced visions while praying. This led me to believe that I really knew what I was doing. After all, I was certainly experiencing deep connections with God and was being wonderfully nurtured and taught. This was about as good as praying could get.

The visions became less frequent, then rare. I still felt deeply centered and connected when praying, and was content. My prayer life when alone and with my fellow Quakers on Sunday mornings was largely the same. Gradually, this shifted. When praying alone, I plumbed the depths. On Sunday mornings, I often sat after my intercessory prayers, unable to still my mind or achieve any depth.

I saw that all the wonderful prayer experiences I'd had were the result of God's work, not mine. I have no idea how to pray. To this day, all I do is show up, pray for others on my list and surrender. What happens, happens.

I have learned that prayer can occur almost anywhere, any time, while we are doing anything. The question of whether a Christian should pray by chanting a mantra is silly. If it doesn't disturb anyone else's prayers, of course they should. Dancing, drumming, singing, chanting are all traditional and wonderful forms of prayer. Who are we to judge or interfere with someone else's soul making connections to God?

A dear form of prayer for me is looking with the eyes of my soul. It doesn't happen often, but occasionally when I am on a prayer walk, I will look at some non-descript object, and it will disappear. I am looking through it to the world of the Spirit. The object has become a window to the other side. Someone standing next to me would be unaware that anything had happened, but I am reassured, touched, taught.

There have been many books written about prayer. I recommend whatever speaks to you. For that is what is correct, at this time. In the future, something else may evolve, showing up in your prayer time. Our intention is paramount. A desire to connect with God and time spent listening, reaching, loving is all that's necessary. The exact form of our prayers is a minor detail. We are creating opportunities for God to work on us. It's God's grace poured out for us during our prayers that will produce the results God intends.

PRAYER WITHOUT CEASING

During a retreat years ago, I mentioned that I wished I could pray without ceasing. I had heard that such a thing was possible. I was directed to the book The Practice of the Presence of God and with some effort, got a hold of a copy. While I loved hearing about Brother Lawrence, I didn't get it. Try as I might, I couldn't figure out how I was supposed to go about praying all the time. I put it on the bookshelf and went about the tasks and roles of my life.

I was leading what I believed was my highest calling – to live my life as a prayer. As many of my deeds as possible were to be acts of love – manifestations of God's presence in my life and the world. I never met this standard, but dedicated myself to it, seeing my work serving children with disabilities as a vocation in the religious sense.

As I neared retirement age, my ties to this work diminished. I was surprised, for I had attempted to be the consummate professional, totally dedicated to my work. Here I was contemplating, then joyfully stepping away from what had been a core of my thoughts, efforts and identity.

I'd had the notion that I could spend more time in prayer. I pondered my future life in retirement. I'd learned the importance of prayer, and concluded that the benefits to the world from another contemplative life was what I was being called to. The thought of serving the world in this way filled me with joy and anticipation.

I was, and continue to be very grateful that I could retire with an adequate pension. Not for me the sack cloth, ashes and utter poverty of medieval mendicants. God has been very gentle with me, and I recognize that few people are in the position that they can devote all their time to prayer. I was in that position, and took up this new task God had put before me.

I prayed all day. Silent prayer that lasted between half an hour and two and a half hours. Three hour prayer walks in parks, at least once a week.

Cross stitching infant's clothes for a homeless shelter and wood carving items to be given away. I wrote a few poems, but stopped doing even this. Except for my leadership position in church, I did no other work.

How strange, and glorious, to know that I was not supposed to be "doing". Instead, God had led me to expend all my energy on "being," "becoming". Removed from my former habitual "I should" caused me to let go. When I sit down to pray I discover all the places I've been holding tight muscles that need to be relaxed. Now, I discovered parts of my life that had been tension filled and that were pulling me away.

Gradually, joyfully, I let go. I didn't have to achieve, didn't have to save anyone. Didn't have to complete lists of tasks or worry about what others would think of my accomplishments.

I was alone, obliged to hang out with God. I reveled in my new life, looking forward each day to how I could spend these wonderful hours. If someone asked me to account for my time, I had little to say. "Did some wood working, took a walk." Not very impressive to others. Boring even.

How wonderful to stand on a snowy hillock, watching chickadees hop about searching for seeds, all the while contemplating God's goodness in providing us with such a marvelous world to live in. To hold a piece of gravel representing perhaps a million years of erosion and to know I am nothing, a tiny speck of the universe, yet so loved.

But people didn't want to hear such things, so I smiled and shrugged that I was keeping busy.

After about six months of this, I noticed a change in myself. I was praying constantly. Even when my mind was taken up with something, deep inside my soul was reaching for God - connected, celebrating.

I'd been obsessed with God for years – my thoughts returning to seeing the Divine in the world around me whenever my attention wasn't demanded by something else. But now, my continual prayers weren't a head thing. This was deeper, steadier, more joyful and more the center of my being. I could think and act without disturbing this process.

This was not the same form of prayer as that described by Brother Lawrence, yet it also is. He talked about frequently using words to reach out to

God. My path was more passive, spending hours resting in God's arms. The results I think were the same – souls forging a connection with God. Tied with bonds of love, far deeper than words can convey.

It flows effortlessly, continually. I have begun to get it, after seventeen years of striving and six months of continual practice. Yet, all that was ever required was for me to let go. I didn't "build" anything, didn't learn a skill. God didn't reward me for having done something right. God had always been there, immediately, immensely, hugely present. Beside me and in me. When I stopped trying to "do" and learned to surrender, I found the One who had always been there.

I'd been surprised when I first retired that I was becoming so passive. The world rewards those who are dynamic and forceful. I had always been energetic and focused on completing tasks. Now, I did very little, and didn't worry about how or if they turned out. I was nudged, guided to become more passive. To be less in control, content with whatever came along.

I'm afraid none of this is going to help anyone else learn perpetual prayer. When I went back and read Brother Lawrence, after I'd begun to "get it", several themes from him resonated.

What this is really about is loving God. Just that. Those who engage in this process to avoid God's wrath or to seek rewards don't get it. Those minor motivations won't get us very far. All that is necessary is love, an overwhelming desire for God. We don't need to learn something or "do". We just turn our face, our hearts, our souls to God and stay there. We may bask in glory or feel only a little tug.

This being a cold climate, one of my favorite forms of prayer was cross stitching on the couch with the winter sun streaming down on me. Accompanied by two dozing cats, I relaxed and settled in. The handwork required enough of attention that my mind didn't wander far. I could be peaceful, resting, and certain of my connection to God for long periods. I didn't learn anything, didn't seem to be accomplishing much.

But I was growing in trust and faithfulness. Most of all, as I made a miniscule effort to reach out for God I was being blessed deeply and gently, aware only of a quiet joy and rightness. I knew I loved those hours and looked forward to them, but couldn't have articulated why.

Looking back, I see those times as part of the fabric of my days that was transforming my relationship with God. Like any relationship, the more time we spend together, the more we gain strength, resilience, depth, affection, and joy. Like tendrils of a vine, my connections grew and grew till I was always connected. My connections not only held me, but nurtured.

Brother Lawrence must have been much further along in this process than I am. He was described as always being peaceful and calm. I am regularly impatient, grumpy and dissatisfied with this and that aspect of my life. Which is OK, for I have lots of room to grow. This is not an all or nothing process. We make a tiny step and meet a huge reward. Then we take another tiny step.

The heart of the process is love. Loving God. For me, prayers of gratitude mixed with efforts to surrender have been the path. I spent many years on what I now see were meditations about God. This was part of processing my epiphany experience –

learning to see the world from the perspective of heaven. These habitual musings taught me a great deal and slowly led me to where I am.

I could have arrived to live in God's heart more quickly if I had added love. My prayers centered on love. The rest of the time, I was operating mostly in my head, trying to understand so I could live rightly. It wasn't until all my time became prayer that I spent enough time loving and developed stronger ties to God. These weren't head efforts, but the surrender of my heart.

How can others, who can't stop virtually all other tasks in order to pray all day achieve this? By going to the center of the task right away. Our attention often needs to be focused on things of this world. Young children continually need their parents. When driving, terrible things will happen if we don't attend to task.

We can find God in those moments when we return to ourselves. Instead of jumping to the next task, we can take a minute to love God. Brother Lawrence's prayers are examples: "My God, I am entirely yours; God of love, I love You with all my heart; Lord, do with me according to Your heart." He goes on to add.. "or some other words which love produces spontaneously." [3]

Even if we don't feel ourselves or our relationship changing, what a wonderful exercise it is to tell God over and over "I love you" each day. And if we do, there's no telling what will happen.

PRAYER AND THIS WORLD

What good is this prayer stuff? It might help the individual praying, but what good does it do the world? Aren't the cloistered lives of monks and nuns irrelevant? In the face of all the world's problems, locking oneself away from the world seems like an act of indifference. Surely we'd be better off if those people came out here and helped.

Not true. Theirs is some of the most important work human beings can do. It's invisible, unknowable, difficult to explain and impossible to prove. A life lived in prayer helps bring God's mercy to this world.

---

[3] The Practice of the Presence of God, Brother Lawrence, Paraclete Press, Brewster, Massachusetts, 1985

God is omnipresent – everywhere, all the time. Just as we are constantly exposed to radio, television and cell phone signals we don't perceive; sound waves that move too slowly and light moving too quickly to sense; we are even more thoroughly immersed in God's presence. Unless our spiritual eyes are open and our hearts attuned, we are utterly unaware of this magnificent force. Moving among and through every particle of all that is, God flows continually. A life lived in prayer synchronizes itself with that presence and by doing so assists.

A metaphor I like involves tuning forks. Although unlike God, for their product – sound waves – is perceptible, tuning forks explain the principals I've learned.

The background tuning fork is God – vibrating at a constant frequency, penetrating every particle of existence. As humans, we are allowed the freedom to vibrate at whatever frequency we choose. An ordinary life vibrates at frequencies different than God's. Some times we're close and amplify Who was already there and sometimes we're very different and reduce God's presence within and around us. Just as sound waves can add together or subtract from each other.

Two tuning forks, vibrating at the same frequency, produce more than twice as much sound. By vibrating in sync, the waves are supported and amplified.

Thus it is with us. When we live in harmony with God, we boost the flow of grace. If we're very contrary, we interfere.

With my spiritual eyes, I've watched the wind of the Spirit blow through me and contemplated for days the implications. My being alters very slightly the character of that wind – pollution isn't the right word, for it is possible for me to have a beneficial effect. We all affect the world around us. Are we contributing our modicum of cleansing, healing and peace to God's presence? Or are we contributing violence and selfishness, thus impoverishing our surroundings?

We can be lanterns, reverently holding as much of the Spirit as we can contain. Or chamber pots, holding the excreta of the worst we can produce. Thus, we can help light the way, or obscure it.

We can be a watering trough, filled with grace and mercy, an oasis for others. Or a desert, pulling the sustenance from those around us.

The choice is ours. We do not have to be physically next to others in order to affect them. Our spiritual efforts reach wherever God takes them. Prayers of union, of supplication, of love are vessels helping to make God's mercy manifest in this world.

I've heard it said, and I agree, that the only hope for this world is for more people to lead lives of prayer. The destruction of societies that were living in harmony with God's rhythms may be part of the reason the world is at so difficult a place now. The Jewish farming settlements on the Stepps of Russia and the Buddhist villages in Cambodia did more than nourish their own members. They were sacred communities that allowed God to be manifest on this earth.

The destruction of their presence, their way of living and relating to each other, diminished all of humankind. Tibetan society, with its marvelously deep connections to the other side, is currently being damaged. Their ability to return to their traditional religious practices should concern us all.

This is not to say that any of these societies were ever perfect. Each had aspects that were only too human, and contained individuals who lived at odds with God's presence. But their norms, their daily practices and rituals were deeply rooted in reverence and connections to each other and God.

What about the Christians? The examples I site were Jewish and Buddhist. Christians have long traditions of small groups, living apart from society in wonderfully spiritual ways. But these were people who left society to live in the desert or a monastery. The Russian Jews and Cambodian Buddhists didn't have to leave society to live in harmony with God. Their society had grown into that condition.

Where does that leave us in our modern, secular materialistic world? Few of us are called or have the opportunity to remove ourselves. Obligations, reality and options relegate us to continue to work at our current jobs, living where we are now. How can we live a life of prayer?

We can learn from Brother Lawrence. He didn't live some fairy tale existence, resting each day on some puffy cloud. Living in a monastery means living in community. Granted, the community is at least attempting to live according to God's purpose, but it is filled with individuals who irritate and intrude on the heaven we would like to be living in. Brother Lawrence was assigned to tasks he didn't like – for years. He had to deal with health problems.

Yet, he lived a life wonderfully grounded in the presence of God. How'd he do that? The same way we can, right where we are. We have to love God. That has to become the center of our reality. More important than the distractions, temptations, frustrations, fears, hurts, pain, loss of daily life. If we can silently offer up a phrase meaningful for us – "God I love you," "Holy Spirit, be with me," and mean it many times a day, we are on the path.

The rest is up to God.

UNITIVE PRAYER

Prayer not only brings mercy to individuals and the world, it also acts powerfully on us. It is a very efficacious way we can grow and be transformed. The image comes to me of a plant that can exist in the shadows, or can be moved about each day to spend some time in the sun. We move out of the shadows of this world to bask in God's glory each time we pray. The more time we spend there, the more we can grow.

A plant doesn't have to strive and struggle in order to grow. Neither do we, if we spend time regularly in unitive prayer. We're not telling God anything, we're not trying to hear any answers. All we want is to be with the One. We act purely out of love. Just to be with the one we love.

It took me a few years to figure out that the best spiritual discipline I could have was daily prayer. At first, these were brief intercessory prayers. As I become more comfortable, the sessions got longer and I found that I was just resting for part of the time. And that was OK. Not much was happening, but it felt good to have this time.

Sometimes a vision would come, but usually it was simply a peaceful, quiet time. I tried to keep my mind empty, resting. When thoughts came up, I would acknowledge them and let them go. It felt like I was being obedient, surrendering.

Perhaps ten years ago, I spent my lunch hour sitting on a bench in the cemetery of the former State Hospital where I had first worked. After my intercessory prayers, which included my former patients, I rested. It was a beautiful spring day and I was comfortable in the sun. I drifted into a period of quiet after my intercessory prayers. When I opened my eyes, 20 minutes had passed.

Had I fallen asleep, warmed by the spring sun? No, it didn't feel like that. I had gone from unaware to fully awake in an instant. There was none of the residual languor the occurred when I woke from a nap. I'd lost those minutes. Was this OK? Had I done something incorrectly when praying? Searching my soul, I found a sense of peace. The term I came up with is that I had a spiritual black out. It felt like God had borrowed my soul, my being for that time. What for, I had no clue.

I continued to ponder this and was a little apprehensive when approaching my prayer time the next day. That day, and for many more, my prayers remained as they had been – ordinary and peaceful. Reviewing what had happened, it occurred to me that this may have been another of God's tests – did I trust enough to hand over my soul? I had.

I became comfortable with what had happened, secure in the knowledge that I had trusted

God, and that the phenomenon – what ever it was – was in keeping with God's purpose. Several weeks later, it happened again for about ten minutes. I re-examined myself. Was this sleep? No, it didn't feel like it. It began to happen more often during my prayers, always ending in time for me to return to work. Was this a form of self-hypnosis, was I somehow controlling when it ended? No, it still felt like surrender.

I talked with several other people living spiritual lives. They suggested that this was a healing process and one involving union with God. That was reassuring, but I had no way to validate their comments. To this day, I have no idea what goes on during those times.

Now that I am retired, I can spend unlimited periods in prayer. Some days, my silent sitting prayers last only twenty minutes, and all that happens is the intercessory prayers that begin each session. Then it feels right for me to get up and be about my more physical forms of prayer. Other days, I barely begin the intercessory prayers before I "come to" and discover that as much as two and a half hours have passed, and I failed to pray for everyone on my list.

There is no sacrifice involved here. I sit in a comfortable chair with as many warm clothes/blankets on me as necessary to keep warm. Mine is not the martyr's path. God is very gentle with me, and my path more nearly represents that of a pampered sloth.

Neither is there ecstasy, for I am unaware. I have developed a deep satisfaction from these periods, for they symbolize for me my willingness to surrender. Deep in my soul, where I can't begin to find words, I recognize that I am joining with the One. That process has been healing and has brought me closer to God through some subtle unknown process. I have long had the sense – the hope? – that God is making use of my soul during those times. What for, I have no idea.

Thus, the simple act of praying daily has transformed my spiritual life. Not through merit. My part was to show up and wait, hoping and wanting to be with. I could promise nothing, demonstrate no accomplishments and was passive rather than striving. I had to accept my brokenness, limitations, faults and foolishness and set them aside, content to sit with heart and soul open.

Brother Lawrence and the lives of the saints make occasional reference to the phenomenon I've labeled spiritual blackouts. None of what I've seen explain how they occur, or what their purpose is. I have no idea how common an experience this is. It appears to me to be a blessing and an outgrowth of the process of daily practicing loving prayers. This unknowable time supports the growth of deep bonds. Truly, the ways of the soul transcend our feeble thoughts and the bounds of our hearts.

DOVE

Sacred Dove
come,
drink from my soul.

I would be a pool
still
pure enough
for you to bathe.

Letting failures,
all outcomes sink,
what can I rise up
for your splashing?

My gifts,
You gave.
I am,
was Yours.

Let us share sunbeams,
a single graceful note,
baby's soft caress.

Alone
unmoving
my life's task fulfilled
if You can bathe and rest.

COMPASSION

I once heard a commentator venomously dismiss a group of "bleeding hearts". I carried that with me in prayer for several days, examining how it struck me and why. I wondered what that person would say if I responded that it was not my heart that bled, but my soul.

I see that we are all one. Moreover, God loves us all equally, cares for us equally. No one is unimportant. No one is beyond redemption or the reach of God's love. No one is deserving of unrelieved suffering, even if they contributed to the circumstances they now are in.

We are all God's children. What a simple statement. What profound implications. God loves each of us infinitely more than humans are capable of loving. If we are to be pale imitations of God, what a great obligation we all have then to love one another. What pain and disappointment we cause in heaven when we fail to care for one another.

Tens of thousands of people die each day from the effects of malnutrition. Millions are hungry. Only those of us who are both blind and deaf can deny that we aren't aware of the appalling conditions of so many of our brother's and sister's lives.

Yet, we blithely go about our lives, concerned whether we can get our hands on the latest, greatest whatever. "Those people" are not me or mine, so I ignore them.

I suspect this is a reflection of our animal selves, combining territoriality with self-interest. A pack of wolves will defend its territory against strangers, preserving its food supply and safety. Some indigenous tribes and early city-states did the same, for the same benefits. There is 'us'. All others are 'them'. For the good of those I am concerned about, I am not and should not be concerned with them. What's good for us, is good. Their problems are just that, theirs.

A number of the life boats from the Titanic were only partially filled. Crews had refused to seek out people in the water for fear of becoming overwhelmed and sinking.

If I am hungry and have only once piece of bread, and you are starving, what should I do? Share and imperil us both? Refuse and allow you to starve?

I must do what is most loving. In some circumstances, it means refusing to give a beggar money, for that encourages dependence and may feed an addiction. If I am able, it could mean sitting down and eating with them. What God wants us to do in each instance isn't clear.

What I must <u>not</u> do is deny their need or their existence. To do so denies part of my existence, and causes me to turn my back on the God that is in them. We typically think of sin as something active, something we deliberately do that alienates us from the One. Far more common is the 'act' of not doing, of turning a blind eye and going about our business.

Nor are we called to make decisions for or do things to others. Instead, we must be with and work with them. It's the difference between pity which says, "I am better off/better than/better able to decide than you. I will give, you will receive and we can then go our separate ways. I will be better off for having been noble enough to help. And of course, you will be grateful for receiving what I provided."

Compassion says instead, "I am with you. I am your brother or sister. Your need is also my need. What can we do together?"

It's easier to pity others than to be with them, especially if we are to accept that they are our equals. Far easier to do for than to do with. Why should we after all? Isn't it enough that I am willing to help?

I was flabbergasted at a conference by the answer of a visitor from East Africa. The question had been posed to him, "If we can raise the money, would you prefer that one of us travels to visit you, or would you prefer that we sent that amount of money to use in your good works?" He replied, "Please come and visit us. More than money, we need to be in community with you."

This, from a man who worked to provide food, shelter, medicine and basic school supplies. Yet, he felt it was more important to make the interpersonal connection between those who had little and those who had much. I had a pretty good idea as well about who would learn and gain the most from that visit.

CALLING

There is a great
great river of pain.

I will not turn my back
nor stand on the bank,
comforting myself
with vicarious glance.

I must not stay dry –
moaning with pity.

I am called to wade in,
immerse myself.
Joining my drop of compassion
to dilute the flow.

What a difference it would make for our lives, communities, country and the world if many people could simply see. Of course I need to share with others. Pay taxes? No problem, if the money was effectively spent to help others. Deny myself? Enlist my family in giving, even if it meant going with less? Yes. Choose to spend my leisure time doing with? Yes, wherever led by God to go.

There is nothing wrong with making money – if no one is exploited. There is nothing wrong with having money. We will however have to account for what we do with the resources God has given us. Typically, we believe that we obtained what we have through our own efforts and thus, deserve them. They are ours, to do with as we please.

This is another fine piece of arrogance. Most people who are successful had a great deal of help in getting there. Those who did it on their own were blessed with the necessary mental and emotional abilities. And where did those come from?

We so easily confuse the ability to do something with propriety. "I can, therefore it is permissible." There are limits of course. Even if we own a gun, we understand that although we could shoot our neighbor, we shouldn't. What we don't see is that if we have the resources to buy something we don't 'need', we should ask God whether we should.

There is nothing evil about new curtains. Buying that which we don't need, and thus denying necessities to an AIDS orphan is wrong. Wrong to the point of sin. Wrong to the point of evil. And virtually every person in the 'first world' has succumbed.

Were we to live as God intends, the first world would be much different. Citizens would work hard, be given resources, then in turn carefully share with those who have less. Luxury goods would not exist, for there would be no market for them. Neither would there be a market for cheap imitations of status symbols.

We would instead understand that our salvation does not lie in possessions. Our joy comes from God, which in turn calls us into community with all souls.

Each of us lives in the palm of God. Every sip of water, every breath was created by God. Life is a gift. The world is a gift, along with everything in it. All we really own are those things we will take with us into the next world – the memories of what we did with what we were given and the time we had. To think we 'own' that book, car, house, whatever is a form of self-deception. If you learn tomorrow that you have terminal cancer, tell me what you truly own. Moreover, tell me what you value. Chances are, you will talk of the relationships important to you. You are blessed if one of those relationships is with God.

BEING TENDERED

There is a rather odd Quaker term that describes what happens when compassion is embraced. We become 'tendered'. To me, it means that we are open to and aware of the condition of others. Rather than ignore and fail to see a homeless person or the woman passing in the grocery store who appears sad or fatigued, we take them into ourselves.

Then we are with them. They are not 'other', their pain and problems are not something we don't have, they are also ours.

How does this work? When I see someone who appears to be in need, I shift into prayer. My soul reaches out to theirs, and I ask for God's mercy for both of us. I am not better than them, am not better off then they are. I am with them, and as much in need of God's mercy as anyone on earth.

What good does that do? Perhaps none, in immediate physical terms. It does open me to be instructed, if God wants me to carry out some task with that person. It puts a look on my face that is more human, and may in itself be a gift. With my spiritual eyes, I see God's grace pouring down on both of us. It already was being poured out for us, but now, our portions are joined. Our souls are joined, even if for only the moment it takes for me to breathe a prayer.

I also become tender hearted, open to the joy and pain of viewing our human condition. As I was processing my epiphany experience, one of the places most difficult for me was the grocery store. My eyes filled with tears as I viewed the silly ways we have made use of the gifts God has given us. So much of what is sold for food is nearly useless or down right harmful. We are so incredibly self-indulgent.

On a deeper level, my soul also became tendered. This was part of my spiritual growth. I spent years looking at, thinking about suffering and contemplating the human condition from the perspective of heaven. I learned that we are all equal and important in God's eyes. I saw that we are all one, and experienced living with all souls in God's heart. Inevitably, my eyes were also opened to the suffering and injustice in this world and I joined with that as well.

To fail to join with the world's pain would have required cutting myself off from the rest of humanity. That is the essence, the basis, of the self-centered life our animal selves lead us to. But at what a price!

This then is a choice we face on the spiritual path. Go back, turn in on ourselves and live selfishly. Or go on, knowing the grace and joy of embracing God while at the same time embracing suffering. Thus, we live a dual emotional life on the trail. Part of me dances with joy, while another part is anchored in pain. Ecstasy and agony. It has always been the way of spirituality.

My prayer life is bordered by both. Sometimes, I walk in joy. Sometimes, I join in suffering. And what good does it do, my walking alone in a park, soul filled with pain? What possible difference can my efforts do to effect the lives of those half the world away?

My soul is joined with theirs, and I am a channel for God's mercy. Our souls are joined, not only on this earth, but with those in heaven as well. To the extent that I can empty myself, turn and deliberately connect with those in pain, I can bring some small measure of solace. Unnamed, unknown, subterranean and impossible to quantify or detect. I am part of all that is, and part of all that could be.

As worthless as this may appear, what if a half – a quarter – of the people in the world spent time every day earnestly praying for those in need, and in the process became tendered?

'VACATION' PHOTO

Sitting on boulder strewn
northern shore.
Breathing with the waves.

I hear your
sighing keening cries
from a thousand miles

and am one
with your pain loss grief.

You were torn burned smashed
for years
by ignorant indifferent cruel.

Released,
your nerve ends –
screaming tentacles – grasp to pass it on.

I,
fool.
Hunch on ancient stone,
taking it all in.
So it won't continue.

DEATH

We come now to a hard subject, one that makes many people uneasy. Do we truly trust God? Believe in his/her goodness? How much? Totally?

Then what is there to fear about death? The transition, yes. Few of us get to choose the circumstances of our deaths, which introduces a huge element of the unknown. Moreover, we'd always prefer to be in control, and here we have little.

Like almost everyone else, I'd prefer to avoid pain and have no wish to linger for months/years barely alive.

But I long for death. Not because I'm depressed, nor because this life is so terrible. I'm impatient. The more I pray, the more I want to be with God. Now. This is not running from, but the ultimate running to. I've glimpsed heaven and was in the presence of that great love that awaits us all. I know that eventually I'll be there forever.

At first, the world of the Spirit was vague, something to be glimpsed briefly and infrequently. Oh, those blessed prayer walks, where the veil would be pulled aside for me and Glory would shine through. Those quiet hours of silent prayer, when God crept into my depths and lingered. Gradually, this world of the senses began to pale. The hidden world took on substance. I lived for years with one foot in each, but now this three dimensional reality pales in comparison. Like an iron filing hurtling toward a magnet, my soul strains toward the One.

For years, one of my prayers has been, "Take me Lord. Let me come to You. I'm tired. How about after I finish this next task you have for me? Oh, and can I skip the pain and lingering part?"

And I'm given another lesson to learn; humbled again and sent on an errand.

Sick, you say? Weird? Well, it's true that longing for death breaks a fundamental norm of typical living. But, it has deep roots in the Christian tradition. A saint's holiness was judged in part by their embrace of death. Many accounts of the lives of saints include details of their deaths – even though these were but brief moments in a full life. Cloistered monks and nuns are said to be very comfortable with death.

A desire to move on is explicitly stated in some hymns. The Sacred Harp hymn I'm Going

Home includes the following lyrics: "Farewell vain world! I'm going home! My Savior smiles and bids me come, and I don't care to stay here long. I'm glad that I am born to die, from grief and woe my soul shall fly, and I don't care to stay here long!"[4]

Granted, life was very difficult in 1850 and death came more often and more suddenly than it typically does now. For a congregation to sing about wanting to leave this life to go home displayed a great trust.

What kind of way is this to live, longing for death?

Glorious!

What shall I fear, when I know that the very worst that can happen is that I will fly into the arms of Perfect Love? This is not a life mired in death and despair, but living anchored in hope. Life lived from the perspective of heaven.

---

[4] I'm Gong Home, Leonard Breedlove, 1850, The Sacred Harp, 1991 Sacred Harp Publishing Company, Inc

Before my epiphany, I didn't think much about heaven. Maybe there was one, maybe I'd go there, probably it will be nice.

Then I experienced heaven. It took years to process, but the reality of heaven became the center of my understanding. While God was taking over my heart and soul, my mind grappled with the implications of what I'd seen.

When I look around now, I'm perplexed that heaven plays such a small part in many contemporary religions and virtually no part in secular society. Many years ago, when death visited often and people knew they had little control over their lives, heaven shone brightly. For most people, it's now vague and barely relevant.

It's my central reality. I will die, and I will go to heaven. Everyone goes to heaven. I need to repeat that, for it is little understood. EVERYONE GOES TO HEAVEN!

We'll talk later about what happens there. It's enough for now to get past the issue of who. I know, you're saying, "What about people who have done evil things? Hitler? Stalin and Mao – those last two didn't even believe in God, and persecuted religious leaders in an attempt to stamp out religion.

What is God? My answer is that God is Perfect Love. What kind of God would send people to earth to live in the body of an animal with limited understanding? Subject to the instincts and drives of a predator? Often struggling with a personal history of abuse and assault? Perhaps further compromised by mental illness or cognitive dysfunction.

And then condemn them because they didn't behave well. Condemn them forever, with no opportunity for redemption.

This is a God I do not know. This is a flawed God, whose love is limited and conditional. One who is capable of an ultimate cruelty.

The God I know is Perfect Love, and loves perfectly – without bounds or limits, endlessly, perpetually, unconditionally. A love so perfect that a lowly person like me (and you) is shown mercy. If all God gave us was justice, there would be no hope for any of us in this world or the next. We have all been given – and we will continue to be showered with – mercy. Love and support but most of all forgiveness, over and over again. We have all known these gifts in this life and how much more will be know them when the veils are lifted from our eyes, and we behold God's majesty?

If we are surely going to heaven, not because we deserve it – for none of us do – then death is nothing to fear. We're human, and can be expected to fret about the unknown, pain and loss of control. We can mourn the loss of contact with those we love, and the things of this world that have given us such pleasure. But there is no reason for fear.

None of this is an approval of suicide or deliberately putting our health in jeopardy. We must always be obedient. Part of that obedience involves waiting until it's our time. Our lives are not ours, but a gift from God. I have witnessed as well the widespread lasting damage caused by suicide.

Neither do I condemn the person who has tried/has succeeded in killing themselves. They are loved. Their lives are embraced by God, and their deaths accepted and mourned when they arrive in heaven.

HUMAN

Help me Lord
for I've fallen
again

and I'm afraid you won't help me up.

Lying face down before you
is perhaps where I should stay.

How many times have I offered
the lame excuse
I'm only human.

Each time you lift me
dust me off
caress me.

I've lost count.

I watched for days last summer
while wind
blew through my soul.

And saw how my being
affects others.

Help me.
Help me Lord.
For I am only human.

I have watched relatives and clients battle terminal illnesses, fighting with every ounce of determination and energy they could muster. Their optimism never faltering, they pushed through one treatment after another entirely focused on beating their disease.

Outwardly, I cheered them on. Inwardly I waited, wordlessly available if they wanted to speak about what would happen if they weren't successful. They didn't want to devote any energy into dying, and they surely didn't have any energy to spare. So I waited, and they died without speaking to anyone about their grief at leaving others behind or their fears of what was ahead.

Modern medicine is wonderful – right up until there's no medical hope. Unfortunately, often neither the doctors, families or patients are imbued with the certainty of God's mercy. Using extraordinary means to prolong a life that will almost certainly end in the near future may – note the caveat – be as disobedient to God's will as a suicide which ends a life too soon.

What does God want is a question that if asked and heeded will guide us through difficult times to Love. What more could we want?

GROAN

One tree leans defeated against another,
both groaning in the breeze.
Death whispers
"Come to me".

Gazing downstream,
mesmerized,
surrendering to the flow.
Soul lunging toward the end.

Called back by duty,
tasks unfinished.
Solaced with beauty
and promise.

ALL WILL BE WELL

I continue to consume violence. Primarily in novels, but also on TV. I've gained some insight about why, but haven't yet grown enough to put it out of my life. That will be challenging, for we are surrounded in the United States with violence as a form of entertainment.

My excuse is that I was physically abused as a child, and continue to carry a reservoir of fear. Despite therapies, prayer, forgiveness and grace, some fear remains. Part of my behavior is habit as well, staying with what is familiar.

Again and again, in various media we see the 'good guy' in peril. The more evil the 'bad guy', the more important it is to see good prevail.

Walter Wink uses the term "redemptive violence" to describe this dynamic.[5] He is a theologian, and actually knows what he's talking about. All I have are the insights gained from watching myself. He provides contexts of ancient myths and global conflict. My focus has been on getting my own act together.

---

[5] The Powers that Be, Walter Wink, Galilee, New York, 1998

From my tiny, ego-centric perspective, I agree with what he proposes. In a contained scenario I get to watch (participate) in seeing virtue triumph. There is an evil I should be angry with, rejecting of. A person who is not one of us, whom I am free to project my anger onto. It just stands to reason, for they're bad.

In the end, good always triumphs. I comforted because I am one of the 'good guys'. Perhaps there's a 'to be continued', but the bad guys never win. I can't recall reading a novel, watching a movie or an episode on TV where the good guys lost and there was no hope of eventual success. Bad guys don't get to mount their horse and ride into the sunset, surrounded by all the dead bodies of every good guy. Can't happen. Sounds graphic, doesn't it? But a lot of movies have ended with the hero striding over the dead bodies of all the bad guys.

Who'd want to watch a movie where the bad guys won? That's not how it's supposed to work.

Therein lies the key to the whole genre. The story doesn't work unless virtue triumphs. We get to exercise our anger and in the end are reassured that all is well. I apparently still need that process. I pray some day I won't.

I feel some hope, for in the real world I sometimes process issues more appropriately than this 'me good, them bad' dynamic. First, I have to recall that I trust God. The outcome , no matter how bad it looks at this moment, must be all right because all things return to God. I recall that there is no 'them'. That's me over there, doing whatever it is I object to. Anger and hatred directed at them is anger and hatred directed at myself. Instead, I must seek out the most loving thing to do, checking with God to make sure I am proceeding as I ought.

I'm at a point where I can sometimes keep this perspective, if I have time. Sadly, my immediate response to injustice is still anger, which triggers that old alienation/blaming scenario. If I can take the situation into prayer, sometimes for days, I might emerge where I wish I could have gone right away.

Others can perhaps afford righteous anger, and can keep their anger righteous. It's too dangerous for me because of the dysfunctional habits I've acquired. While I must not accept injustice, my response has to be grounded in love. Otherwise, I get lost and waste emotional energy.

I wonder whether I will live long enough to get past my childhood. The task in this case is to reduce my need for distraction and reassurance that good will prevail. As I have with so many issues, I need to reach down into my depths and lift aspects of myself up so they can be examined. Denying or trying to suppress them doesn't work for long. Only when I face them, acknowledge that indeed they are part of me and go so far as embracing my brokenness, can I get past and let go.

There is little justice in this world. Bad, terrible things happen. How will we respond?

One of my treasured memories is of a brief incident that occurred while I was helping pick up trash along a county road. Our school had signed up to clean highways. I had a half mile to walk by myself. It was late fall, and this stretch wound past several corn fields. I ambled along, eyes on the ground, feeling just fine. A light breeze caused the leaves of the corn plants to clack together. Suddenly, through the noise of the leaves I heard, "All will be well". I'd had enough experience to know right away that I was hearing God's voice.

This occurred at a time I wasn't in desperate need of being comforted. It just happened. Perhaps I've remembered it so vividly because it was purely a gift. Unbidden, unexpected, something for the future. Something to treasure.

It has become one of my touchstones and I ponder it, carrying it with me in prayer. 'All will be well.' Along with the phrase, 'God loves you', it's all the food my soul should need to sustain itself.

As bad as the last century was, the easy part of living on this planet is coming to an end. It's unlikely that technology will be able to create enough water and clean air to allow us to continue to do as we wish. Neither human wisdom nor compassion appear adequate to develop long term solutions that will enable all of us to continue living. They never have, for the poor continued to suffer and die even in the best of times.

When difficulties visit us, some get stuck in, "It's not fair", some in "It's their fault", many in "I want". If I'm where I should be, I can respond, "All will be well." In the face of evil, disaster, pain, or injustice this seems ridiculous. In human terms, it is. If I follow up by praying for mercy and guidance about what I should do, then all for me is well.

If I suffer, and it's unavoidable, this life is short. It won't last forever. If death strolls up and waits in the corner, that's all right for I see death as a door, not an abyss. Everyone, and ultimately, everything returns to God.

I recall the sandstone cliffs from the park I walk in, laid down 400 million years ago. I am a speck, utterly insignificant in the vast universe. I am also God's dearly beloved child. I lived in God's heart before I was born, live now in God's palm, and will return joyously to live in God's presence forever.

Death is God's final gift to us in this life.

GALE

Face the gale
till the wind
turns blood red,

looking out over the apocalypse.

As we have lived
by the natural law
so shall we all die.

Our panting,
grasping effort
of preservation
generating boundless hatred,
hastening
the end.

God will grieve,
collect the remains
and grant some other creatures
freedom.

And I pray,
more wisdom.

SUFFERING

God has no use for your suffering. How could it possibly benefit him/her? All that God needs is your attention. The suffering people of this world need your compassion. If you suffer, it is the consequence of the natural world and our human condition. While God doesn't need your suffering, it's possible that others in this world do, for it provides opportunities.

If you've been traumatized, I'm sorry. I pray for your healing. If you're addicted, God loves you, needs and wants you free and able to help others. If you're ill or disabled I pray you get the assistance you need. There is work for you both during your illness and recovery. God is with those who are hungry or seek shelter and hope.

God didn't cause your suffering. Life – and your fellow human beings – did. The human part is easier to see. What would the world look like if we all did our best to care for ourselves and do the work God gave us, and expended all the resources we could on helping each other? If compassion was the norm and wisdom prevailed?

There would be very little hunger, much less disease and universal – world wide – education and health care. Environmental destruction, water shortages, unsustainable population growth, epidemics, habitual hatreds and conflicts would be minimized.

Unrealistic? Ridiculous? My point is that these issues are controlled by humans. If the world is a mess, it's because of our collective failures. God didn't do that. I believe God is waiting to see whether we will gather enough wisdom before it's too late. These horrendous huge problems are opportunities – clarion calls that all is not well. Selfishness, both individual and national got us where we are, and will only make things worse.

God is love. God is mercy, and never causes harm. God allows bad things to happen. That's the deal, made before each of us was born. You might not remember, but you agreed to the circumstances of your life before you were born.

Think of the vulnerable – living in poverty on the river bank or coast, aborted, abused, powerless, mentally disabled, terminally ill. Innocent. What are we to make of their lives?

Many of us have a horrible and inappropriate instinct to assign blame. The reason 'those' people (meaning anyone in difficulty) are ill, hungry, poor, abused, disabled and so on is because it's their fault. What a great rationale for it makes us different, and thus unlikely to share the same fate. It distances us from 'them' and makes it easier to go on to say, "Since it's their fault, I have no responsibility to help".

There's a powerful blend of our fear and selfishness driving this philosophy, with some of that ancient tribal 'us vs. not us' added. Fear because we don't want to share their fate. We don't want to acknowledge that we could end up in the same condition when in fact, disasters, illness, trauma or unemployment could do just that. It's safer to push this awareness away by denying it has any place in our world.

Selfish because blaming frees us from having to devote any of our resources – time, attention, talents, possessions or money – on someone who doesn't deserve it.

What we fail to see is that the things we have are gifts God gave us. I've known very few people who heroically overcame terrible odds to become successful. Working in schools, I was surrounded with staff who had been born with above average academic ability, supportive families and enough resources to attend college. They were average in appearance and healthy.

Yes, they had to comply with expectations as they were attending school, and had to apply themselves. But how hard was that, really? We lavish some of the greatest rewards based solely on how a few people look. Surely that's entirely God's gift, as is the talent that allows the one person to excel among the thousands who practice.

We who are so proud of our accomplishments are exercising just that, pride. Few of us, if we were born with limited resources or faced great adversity would do very well.

And what of the innocent? The birth of children with handicaps puts this blaming screed to shame. Even if someone stretched the limits of reason by blaming the parents, a lack of medical care or maternal nutrition, the child's innocence can not be denied.

It was said in the past that the sins of the parents are visited on their children. Oh no! Don't even try to go there. That would be an exercise in Divine cruelty and injustice. That's not possible and not at all in keeping with the God I know.

I was privileged to serve children with disabilities for thirty years. That gave me a lot of time to ponder questions their lives posed. After a very long time in prayer, I came to understand that we agree to the circumstances of our lives before we are born. Some people agree to be born in need, or become needy.

What's the point? Why should anyone be born into difficult lives? A part of this is the natural law, which includes diseases and genetic variations, some of which create problems. The larger answer is in the opportunities for service these vulnerable lives provide.

In a world where everything was perfect and no one ever needed help, we would all be selfish. We'd never have to be concerned with anyone else. Instead, we live surrounded by an abundance of needs. The question for us is which tasks we are supposed to address.

WHAT ARE WE DOING HERE?

I've been told by some that even asking about the meaning of life is silly, for there is no answer. From the perspective of heaven, I developed an understanding. We are here to be agents of God's mercy. That implies listening to God and acting as we should. It very often means serving others.

This is not some grim, joyless sentence to a life of misery. God is often very gentle, making allowances for our humanness. It's (probably) OK to go water skiing, take a vacation or read a book for enjoyment. Perhaps God approves big things like falling in love, or something as minor as taking a nap.

Of course, we are free to do as we wish. If our choice has been to surrender the freedom that comes with life on earth in order to live a Spirit-led life, then we have to keep checking to see whether this or that is in keeping with God's wishes.

Taking a nap? Does God really care about something so unimportant? Even such a minor issue gives me the opportunity to remember that God loves and cares for me. I should love and care for myself. At my age, and during my retirement, naps can be a good thing. However, I must not use them to avoid doing other tasks that I have been called to.

These internal machinations are themselves a form of prayer, bringing me back to a focus on God. As such, they aren't silly or meaningless. If I weren't such a block head, perhaps I could stay tucked in God's heart with less effort. I'm profoundly grateful for all the activities that help me stay centered. How much more joyful is a trip to the grocery store or a nap, after I've been reminded that God loves me and will watch over me!

Frequently asking whether I should do this or that helps me be available to be used by God. I'm not one of those people who stride across the world's stage in larger than life roles. My experiences usually involve assisting one person at a time, often anonymously or in ways they may not recognize.

I see God's hands at work in this world every week. Frequently this involves someone receiving assistance at a particular moment. Pushing a grocery cart out of the way of an older person who is struggling, then making eye contact and smiling provides affirmation. If done with love, both are nurtured.

How did those two people end up together at precisely the right time? You could say chance. I've been both the helper and the person helped many times. These brief encounters fill me with awe and gratitude.

Under all this activity is the prayer that I am continually called to, seeking to bring another measure of God's presence to this world.

Contrast these largely invisible tiny efforts as the basis for living with societies' usual goals. Ask a group of high school students what they want out of life, and you'll see what we espouse – money, status, possessions, power, sex, fame. Watch prominent people stream across the TV screen – prominent because they have amassed some of those things.

They are on TV because so many of us desperately wish to be like them. To possess scads of whatever. No matter that these are idle dreams, when we subscribe to possessing, desire is what sustains us. Desire is what sustains those on the spiritual path as well – a longing to love and be with God.

The contrast is as stark as can be. Why do I put one foot in front of the other? To get, or to give?

Blessed are those who seek to serve in anonymity, for God will put them to good use.

ANGELS

There is a word for agents of God's mercy – angels. Does this mean that our purpose on this earth is to be angels?

Yes, it does. I have both been served by people who acted as angels, and have served others in that role.

Years ago, our church was asked to support a woman who was coming into town to anonymously donate a kidney. Two days after her surgery, several of us gathered in her room to pray with her. Afterwards, I prayed briefly with her while she laid her hands on mine. With my eyes closed, I 'saw' her wings. They were large and strong. She was an angel.

I went away in wonder, and looked around with my spiritual eyes. I saw that I had wings as well, as did all the others in the circle as we worshiped on Sunday, and finally, everyone. Some have wings that are well developed, others hide and deny theirs. But we all have that potential, the calling to be angels.

One year, I volunteered to serve a significant role in my church's national gathering. This was going to be a difficult task for me. A woman I'd only seen once reassured me at the original meeting, and 'happened' to sit near me at the next two meetings over the next year. As a person, her presence was unremarkable, and I don't remember her name. She helped quietly, unobtrusively. Yet her continued connections with me made it clear that God was holding me very tightly.

At a church conference several years later, I offered my dorm room to a participant who was sleeping in her car. She seemed grateful, and accepted. I moved to a different room where there was an empty bed. When she saw me the next day, she didn't seem to recognize that we'd ever talked. I'd been an anonymous angel for her.

Many of the reports we hear about encounters with angels include contact with a stranger who miraculously says or does something that averts a disaster, and then disappears. Were they real? Were they from somewhere else? Or were they one of God's obedient servants?

But aren't angels supposed to be the embodiment of holiness, pure and unstained with the dregs of this life? Perhaps there are some such in heaven, but I didn't encounter them. Instead, I see that I am surrounded with humans as flawed as myself, who none the less have the potential for great good.

We don't need to be perfect to serve others. We just need a good heart, and humble soul that basks in God's light. Our meager efforts are enough. After all, we don't have to be in charge. God's doing the heavy lifting, and we're just cooperating.

Will these encounters happen often? Can we make it more likely that either we will be helped by an angel, or be used as one? That's up to God. Some helping professions – health care and education – lend themselves to frequent acts of mercy. Everyone has the opportunity to make themselves available, often in the most unlikely places.

We may well not even know the effect that something as small as a smile or silent prayer has on another. And that's all right too, for we're not in this for the rewards, but the service.

If our highest calling is to be agent's of God's mercy, then there must be those who need mercy. That leads us back to the earlier discussion of suffering.

SUFFERING ANGELS

The lives of saints contain some accounts of embracing suffering. This seemed to be part of medieval Catholic holiness. I certainly am in favor of coming to terms with our own suffering, and working to transcend it. We can do incredible things if our minds, emotions and spirits turn to overcoming pain and suffering, rather than expending our efforts in fear and a vicious cycle of self-absorption.

On a broader basis, I see that suffering can be a vehicle to turn us toward God, reaching out for the mercy we so desperately need. Being dependent and helpless is a very meaningful way to approach the One.

I've developed a variety of back problems which limit my activities. They serve to channel me to the tasks God now has for me. They're different from the tasks I had when younger. If I had remained physically capable, chances are I wouldn't have spent months doing nothing but praying. Recreation and volunteering would have been too attractive.

While we can do what we can to minimize and make use of our pain, there is another side to suffering. As different and unnoticed as the back side of a mirror, those who suffer and are in need provide opportunities for others to be merciful.

Personally, this can grate on me. I was the care giver, now I sometimes need help. My children now have to watch out for me, and sometimes step in while I sit idly by. Yet, this allows them to be attentive, generous and compassionate. My infirmities are minor and the result of age. Far larger are the needs of the innocent.

In the dynamic of one who needs, and one who provides care, which person has contributed more? From our human perspective, we would say the person who could have done something else, but chose to help was more noble. Furthermore, when our judgmental arrogance kicks in, we're apt to disparage the unfortunate. We may say, "How wonderful that there are people who stoop to help such as those."

But what if, as I have seen, those in need agreed to the circumstances of their lives before they were born? Were willing to be mentally ill or disabled, poor, oppressed, abused? All so that others would have an opportunity to grow into holiness through service? Then who has contributed more?

Clearly, the homeless alcoholic has given up more than the volunteer who's come to serve him supper. "Wait a minute!" I can hear some say. "That guy's behavior led him to the problems he has. Surely that makes him guilty."

Guilty of what? Poor choices, yes. He is responsible for helping himself – in fact, unless he takes responsibility he will never gain control of his life. But I won't condemn him. I have no idea what contributed to the choices he made. In any case, he is a beloved child of God, and God dwells within him.

My only questions are, "What is the most loving thing I can do?" and "What does God want me to do?" His needs are what speak loudest. Ragged and unkempt, awkward and inconvenient, those in need in our neighborhood, society and the world serve as challenges to all of us who have resources.

Will we help them, as completely as we would if we knew God was standing at our shoulder? Acknowledge God's presence within them? Or refuse – as we usually do - to even see them?

They are why we are on this earth and represent our chance at salvation. We are not here to get, but to give of the talents and resources God gave us. Yes, we can live an affluent, consuming life style, but should we?

I have come to understand that the lives of those in need are more in keeping with God's desire than mine. The more difficult and innocent their lives, the more God honors them. The severely disabled, hopelessly mentally ill, and AIDS orphan are angels. Not because of what they do, but who they are. Instead of being ignored, feared and despised, I should recognize, honor and serve them.

Suffering that isn't – or can't be – relieved in this world makes no sense. The circle is only completed when we return to heaven.

HOMELESS

Wolfing food
outside a Chinese take out.

Shoulders, knees,
hunched.
Gaping fly revealing
underwear is superfluous.

You glance,
eyes red rimmed,
fierce.

And we survey
the contribution
each of us made
to the state you're in

Your part active
mine passive

Forgive me.

HEAVEN

Heaven. If we believe in an after life, that's where we want to be. Long ago, when death was more familiar, heaven was important. Often written and sung about, elaborate scenarios were written about what it would be like. What I've experienced of heaven was not what I expected.

I walked away from my epiphany experience with two truths: God is perfect love, and heaven is forever. Seemingly simple, I still cycle back to contemplate the implications of each.

The easiest to grasp is that heaven is never ending. Until I experienced it, those words had little meaning. Nothing on earth is forever. Everything here dies, wears out, evaporates. Forever. Incredible. On and on and on and on.

The central reality of heaven for me was being in the stupendous presence of God. Imagine standing as close to the sun as we are to the moon. Everywhere you looked, your vision would be filled with fantastic light shows. The heat would be unbelievable, overpowering.

Now, think of standing that close to Perfect Love, a presence more overwhelming than the sun would be. We are spirits in heaven, God is spirit, so we are entirely penetrated, surrounded, suffused, saturated with love. Forever. Any other aspects of heaven are minor when compared to the incredible love given to each of us.

The portion of love we are given in no way diminishes the whole. Nurturing, glorious love is poured out for us in abundance. There are billions of souls past and present, but God loves us individually, personally.

This continual central reality will be the core of our experience. I learned about other aspects of heaven that were not as blissful.

No one deserves this great gift. We humans have some odd attitudes toward heaven. Some religions are exclusive, "Only those who believe and act as we do will go to heaven." There is an underlying accompanying belief, "Those people will suffer while we who are among the chosen won't have to answer for our failings."

The souls of still born children, animists, pagans, atheists and communists are in heaven.

Whatever the exclusive religion, these people were never exposed to it. To imply that God wouldn't welcome them home makes no sense.

Wishful thinking has been taken to its highest peak with the belief that we won't have to answer for our behavior. On earth, we can see and understand little. If human beings have an infinite capacity, it's self-justification. We can always find excuses for what we did and didn't do. We're so good at it, we convince ourselves.

We also can't see very far, and rarely are confronted with the full effects of our actions. Not so in heaven. Our sight and understanding will be restored. We will recall everything we have done, and will see the consequences as they rippled out. Unlike our present lack of awareness, we will not be able to rationalize away either our actions or what we caused. We're stuck with what we've done on this earth.

This is not what we'd prefer. It would be nice to leave the mistakes, omissions, failures and harm we caused behind; along with any responsibility. But that wouldn't be reasonable. There is little justice on earth, but there is in heaven.

Part of the reason everyone goes to heaven is that all are confronted with their earthly lives. Forever. There is no need for a hell where sins are paid for. We all pay for the poor behavior we all indulged in while on earth.

Behind all this is God's tremendous love and forgiveness. Otherwise, heaven would be eternal misery. Those who spend their lives fearing God's punishment have it partly right. They will be punished, but it will be by their own awareness.

We also see all the good we generated. Heaven is a social place, where we are connected with the souls of all those we loved, hated, helped, feared, harmed and ignored.

I'm aware that I will spend eternity next to the souls of third world children whose lives were shortened by starvation. We all will, for there are plenty of such souls to go around. The arrogance and blindness that led us to ignore the needs of others will result in our being connected to those who were harmed by our indifference.

"Wait a minute!" I can hear people say. This isn't at all what I want. I want heaven to be pure joy, undiluted ecstasy.

You don't deserve it. None of us do. God gave us our freedom to live as we wished while we were on earth. When here, we are influenced by our animal shells, but this didn't give us license to live selfishly. We have the chance to transcend ordinary living and seek holiness. If we do that, we'll know more bliss and less pain in heaven. The reverse is also true.

Heaven will be what it will be, and life in this world is what it is. How can the existence of heaven affect our daily lives?

The existence of God and the assurance of heaven is the center of my reality. I used to smile when I saw the phrase 'no fear' used as a marketing ploy. For what is there to fear, when I know that the worst that can happen in a given situation is that I will die, and return to be caressed by a loving God?

That assurance supports my understanding that 'all will be well'. Of course everything will turn out all right, for everything returns to God. In the end, we all die and go to heaven. Will we treat others with love; and when we need help, will others assist us? Are we willing to spend a significant portion of our resources on the tasks God assigned us?

Everyone won't behave lovingly. Mother nature can be indifferent and capricious. We will face adversity. What are we to do? Ask for guidance and seek for the most loving response, secure in the knowledge of God's mercy.

Things may not turn out on this earth as we would like. Our child's cancer may progress, we may lose our job and with it our dreams. As difficult as it can be to swallow this life's cruelties, there is hope, and work for us all.

It might not seem to make sense to look for what we're supposed to do about a terrible circumstance. Can't we just be miserable and overwhelmed that our child's life is in danger? Of course we will, but how tragic if that's the only outcome. The child loses their future and the lives of family members are diminished.

Often, years afterward, people will relate how they were able to turn a tragedy into a positive. Remember, God didn't give that child cancer. Nature did that – one of the terrible consequences of living on this wonderful earth. Tragedy is an opportunity for all those it touches.

Each moment of every day, we decide. Some people have little control of their thoughts or emotions. For the rest of us, there are choices. Choose joy, gratitude, obedience, love? Or allow the world around me to dictate how I react – with fear, anger, sorrow? If I'm hurt, will I respond in kind, or respond as God wishes?

How will I wish I had lived, when I have to spend eternity reviewing everything I've done?

Thank God for mercy, now and forever.

NIRVANA

If you jumped ahead to this chapter because you want to experience heaven on earth, I'm sorry, but you can't have it. You'll first have to get out of your own way. We can know heaven on earth only when our souls – our wills – are attuned to God's. It requires submitting completely out of love, without regard for reward.

Thus, when we are content to simply love all that is the way it is, including letting go of our intense desire to be with God, we find ourselves surrounded with bliss. God won't pick you up until you're content with not being picked up. When we fill ourselves with love, only love, we find we are also immersed in it.

I have known this for one afternoon, and brief moments since. As I began my prayer walk that day, my heart was filled with joy. Fall sunlight filtered down through multi-colored leaves. Seeds of various weeds floated, gleaming as they gently drifted, twirled and sank to their new homes. The stream quietly burbled, carrying fresh-dropped leaves, each one a tiny boat. Some glided out of sight. Others piled up on rocks, were caught by a protruding branch or submerged to roil underwater.

My soul expanded, flowing up the hills and encompassing all that I could see. I was fully there, in those moments. More than accepting; loving all that this existence holds. Pain, loss and suffering. My failings. Birth and death, evil and holiness. I was one with it all, the ugly and sublime.

God's love poured down upon me. I was one not just with all that exists in this world, but with heaven as well. Relaxing, grateful, I wandered through the park for hours. Thinking no deep thoughts, making no great effort. Blessed.

Since that wonderful afternoon, I have had only glimpses of perfection on earth. It seems that I'm not able to keep myself balanced for any length of time. Still, I smile each time I think back to those hours, happy with the promise of what awaits me. Perhaps that was the purpose of that first afternoon – to allow me to bathe in splendor, creating a memory I can cling to. I travel through this world, content to listen and love, knowing I have much to learn, and much to do. Occasionally I step, however briefly, behind the veil. If only others could see, that to die to self is to gain all.

I will know that I have died to myself when I can say with no reservations, "Thy will be done." This requires complete trust in God – a God I know is all powerful and loving. A focus on heaven is the only way I can come to grips with the pain, injustice and limits of this world. Eternal bliss is the only salve for the monstrosities nature and we humans inflict on each other. I must also give up all my wants, which anchor me to this reality. It's so frustrating to repeatedly see myself mired in longing for comfort, intimacy, recognition, security. God has provided me with all those things, yet I want more, not only from God or in the future, but now, from my fellow humans. My wants can never be fulfilled. The act of wanting leads only to brief satisfactions followed by more longing. The only rational course is to first learn to be content with what God has provided. If I can then go on to let go even of this, and want only to love God, then I can know bliss.

How can I give up wanting? First, I must acknowledge what I'm feeling. Ignoring or denying what's going on inside myself wastes energy in suppressing and containing feelings that will continue to grow, albeit in the dark. Pulling them up and facing them, knowing them for what they are is a first step. Then, I must accept that this is part of me at this moment. Medieval saints punished themselves severely to rid themselves of temptations. A more humane approach is to love myself. Only by embracing these feelings, perhaps with sorrow and regret, can I gain dominion over them. And then I have to let them go, for I realize that they can not be fully or permanently fulfilled. Desire leads only to unhappiness.

The great irony that wanting God, as laudable as it is, contains elements of selfishness is the last barrier I need to overcome. Some traditions overcome wanting with a years-long great effort of will. My path has been passivity, learning to let go and wait. Perhaps if I sit quietly often enough with my heart open, God will again fill my soul to overflowing.

Do I deserve such great gifts? No, we flawed humans can't possibly deserve God's love. As has happened so often, my puny efforts to reach toward God will be returned a million fold. But this must be an exercise in pure love. Reaching for God because we fear punishment will gain us reassurance. Doing good in order to earn rewards either in this life or the next will be acknowledged. Only when we love heedlessly, recklessly, helplessly will we be soaked in grace.

We love because we love and can't see beyond that. What is there to see beyond God?

Buddhists achieve something of this through the exercise of letting go and accepting this existence as it is. While that was a necessary part of my learning, I had the great benefit of God's presence teaching me, consoling, forgiving, challenging and loving me. I'm much too lazy to climb mountain tops. Thank goodness, heaven came to me.

My part has only been little acts of love. Turning to God, reaching, longing, leaning. Standing up, head hung and shamefaced when I've messed up again. Recognizing my helplessness, weakness and need. Being content to wait, for years if necessary. Practicing trust. Being humility. Rejoicing in lessons learned, and clinging to graces given to sustain me.

Throughout, God never moved away from me, never failed to provide me with what I needed to grow – challenges I could (barely) handle, enough wisdom to understand, love always.

Lives lived in love are their own reward. Lives lived in love will be rewarded.

CONCLUSION

Writing all this was at first daunting but became instructive. I was often surprised by what showed up on the page. I spent most of my effort keeping my daily life deep and centered, preparing myself to come to these hours. It became a form of prayer and great joy.

Knowing that I will spend eternity with the souls of those touched by these words fills me in ways I can't express. How wonderful it will be to commune with each other!

I have a request, for those of you who are healthy enough. More than 60,000 people wait on lists for kidney donations. They represent one of the few chances you have to literally save someone's life. If you donate, it will cost you several month's recovery. That's all. The pain was minimal, the care extraordinary. What – if any – relationship you have with your recipient is up to you.

When I donated a kidney anonymously, I didn't do it for that particular person. How could I? I'd never met him, knew nothing about him and didn't meet him until a year afterward. We correspond now once or twice a year, and visit when he comes to town for a checkup. I did it as a response to nudges from God. Looking back on it four years later, it gives me a sense of confidence because when God called, I was able to say, "Here I am. Take me." Perhaps I will have the courage to continue putting one foot in front of the other, spiraling always toward the One.

Are you so called? Please tuck that question in your backpack as you continue on your spiritual path. Contact a large transplant center if that's where you're led.

God Bless,

Mike

SINGING

singing, singing

through my chores
a million yells for dad
my daily work routines

singing, singing
grace is singing

through failure and rejection
disappointment and despair
love and triumph

singing, singing
grace is singing

with all that I see
each task that I do
and all that happens to me

singing, singing
grace is singing
singing in my soul

ANVIL CHORUS

Lay me on the anvil Lord
and beat hell out of me.

If I'm not forming fast enough,
stuff me into the fire.

Give those bellows several woofs
till I'm translucent red.

Then grab that big ol' two pound sledge
and have at me again.

Slag will surface, sparks will fly
and I'll start taking shape.

Then when I finally get to where
I'm doing what you want.

Plunge me in the waiting tub
I'm quenched in sacred love.

So tempered that my being rings
a joyful song of thee.

SING

Having felt a breath of air
as the hem of God passed,
I will not sing your song.

Especially I will not, for those that
went before.

I have seen them rise up
on a still spring dawn,
to drift as ground fog
over the cemetery wall
whispering
"Why".

I know it's a comfort to belong;
pride of prevailing,
security of strength,
tradition after all.

But my heart aches
and I cannot join you
singing happily of war
in the Star Spangled Banner.

STEPPING STONE

Perhaps if I went into
the backyard,

reached down with both hands,
and pulled myself underground
till only the top of my head
stuck out

and stayed there several life-times,
I could get rid of this self.

Maybe dirt can cure myopic vision
stop up a prideful mouth.

Protruding skull could be useful
as a stepping stone.

Say, didn't I see one of those
the other day?

LOVE

These eyes have never seen You
                    my love,
and I know they never shall.

I am content to contemplate
the merest glimpse of you;

reflection of a buttercup,
dew drop's gleam,
green of a hillside painted with a forest.

I will look for You with my heart,
where I see You shining
through a million suns.

Nor will this skin be touched.

But my soul,
what you've done.

I'm immersed in a Love
bigger than time
past space.

My every particle
infused, saturated.

love
comfort
peace
grace

You.

AFTER

After I grovel
and plow a furrow with my forehead
for decades

to balance.

Then

lay me on the prairie

so the wind
        curves into eye sockets
        streams between bleached ribs

        hymn singing,

        and spreads my remains

till each square mile of earth
contains a molecule.

That of me added to Who was
already there.

BAGGED

I
human
bag of sacred fluid.

You
all compassionate
God.

Skewer me
with foibles great and small.

I love to slide
and glide past.

But that doesn't get me
very far.

Better that I stand

oozing

focused

growing.

US

Old friend
your words of last night
lie heavy between us.

I heard
your desire to bring violence
to those people.

I also heard
your fear.

You are my brother
I love you
and am with you.

Yes.

I am their brother
love them
and am with them.

So when you go to harm them
I must be the first.

Bring your
insults
blows
death
to me.

I will be there
hands empty
arms open.

You can not love another
without loving me.

You can not harm another
without harming me.

HANDS

Your eyes reflect
the flames of hell.

Pain has frozen
your gaze.

Let me step between.

I do not fear
your agony.

I have had
my own.

Fresh come from bathing
with moonlight,
I bring you
cloud tops
to soothe your brow.

Not yet nothing,
I can do little.
But having served
as sunlight for centuries,
and generations
as slaughter house drain,

I bring you these hands,
wrapped in solace.

Come.
Lie on the universal web
and seek healing.

RIDGE RIDER

Ridge rider.
Mounted on misery.
Cloaked in Comforter.
Tracing boundaries
between this watershed
and that.

Seeking.
Scanning chasms.
Prayer unceasing.
Fearing only abandonment.

Silhouetted.
Exposed to gales.
Inviting others.

Huddling, only eyes exposed.

Rejoicing.

FALL

Wind
shuffles fallen leaves.

Each individual,
helpless;
clatters, No!

I, unique
must have a way
to control the wind.

Prayers and incantation
sacrifice and promises.

The wind
shuffles fallen leaves.

TURN

Turn away from me my
Love, or let
me leave this life.

My soul, bound
and weighted,
can not contain
enough of You.

If You leave, life
will end. If You
stay, I'll die of joy.

Go just a little
step, and fix Your
gaze another place.

Then I can dare to
look again, breathe
and reach for You.

SER 1

At the top
of the sacred fire's plume

smoke blends with the cosmos.

There!
There we have been,
are
and will be.

Souls singing
dancing
radiant.

As water
and fish
we are one.

As earth
and buffalo,
we are one.

As air and bird,
we are.

We are
each

standing on trust,
flying on love.

Pulse universal –
be and not be
open and closed

you and I
yes and no.

all
all
one
one

one.

HIDE

So, who's going to explain?

They won't believe me,
even if I'm able to speak.

So, I hope I never
collapse in public
from adoration of You.

My downcast eyes
hide tears of joy
gathering in the corners.

I'm trying
to live
normal
in the world.

But it's getting so hard
when Love breaks through.

VEILED

were that there
was a hole

torn in the veil

so I might glimpse

but I would not be content
even then

nor will
ever be

till you draw back that veil

and welcome me home

TEMP

Cursed temptation
leaving me writhing on the dirt,
loathing myself.

Blessed temptation
tormentor
teacher
springboard.

Poor human,
I must embrace agony
        to find ecstasy.
Face ugliness
        to see beauty.
Know I am nothing
        to be given everything.

Dear God, You
lift me up as a loving parent,
embrace me
then set me down again.

And as a little child filled love,
I turn away to play and learn and run.

But I am not a child
and Your great gifts require all of me.

You belong
on the front of my heart
and lips
and mind.

Would that I could hold you there
with joy.

I cannot.

WAVING

I stand on the shore of the ocean,
ecstatic,
wrapped in the pulse of
        the universe.

It is from here
we came.

And at the other end of these
                waves
God's heart beats.

I am a drop of water.
Helpless.
Invincible.

EMPTY

Empty.

I would empty myself
of self,
plastering residuals
against inner periphery.

hollow
shell

capsule
carrying
You.

BECOME

I sit beneath the weight of my world
paralyzed

will I ever learn humility
am I enjoying it too much

what is this drive to
teach
share

does it differ
from the flapping of one more
old guy's gums

step forward
step back
sit and don't move

if only
if only I could get it just right

get what
how

mayhap I will do my wont
while resting on a boulder's sunny side
and be
just be

till I become

SECRETS

beneath the brook's murmurings
voices
offer secrets

peace
joy
serenity

hiding in plain sight

waiting
for those

who turn away
see through
reach beyond

WORSHIP

Closing my eyes
I rest in the arms of the Lord.

Quiet settles
stirred by the rustling of angels.

Expectant silence
waits to hear again
the word of God.

In community
celebrating
this taste of heaven.

IMPLACABLE

barely frozen stream
wears pristine coat

current
silent
hidden

born of storms long ago
absorbed

flowing underground

seeping
joining unnoticed

glimpsed where
surface turbulence roils

gliding quickly under

unseen
implacable

COLD

night ice
creeps
toward tumbling water

cold seeps deep into
rocks
trees
bones

a malignant force
driving life
into hiding

between stars
deep space

dark nothingness

essence of the universe

this biting cold
but a faint reflection

yet with sunlight
ice rime

retreats

EYES OF MY SOUL

with the eyes of my soul I see

a sunlight bathed curtain

exquisite

simple objects
leaf
twig
last year's weed

windows

STONE TRAVEL

If you would know the universe
travel through a stone.

Feel its borders from within
taste its minerals.
Inventory atoms,
recalling where each has been.

Then you will find
outside the bounds,
the center.

And you will know
we are one
and have been
before time
before space

and shall be one again
after we account
for where we've been.

.

STEEL WIND

Steel wind
blowing through,
drags my soul
downstream.

While healing,
I bleed.

Rejoicing,
yet weep.

Shimmering arabesques
dance on hill tops

becoming.

Come

be.

BOUND

Feet.
Why do I have to have feet.

If I could but reject these feet
and fly.

You will not allow it.

I understand.

But it groans
being earth-bound.

Forced to serve
earthly tasks
in public.

Can I serve only
in hidden silence?

OK, OK
I'll go back and get them.

Made in the USA
San Bernardino, CA
10 January 2016